NATO at 70

Keith Hartley

NATO at 70

A Political Economy Perspective

palgrave
macmillan

Keith Hartley
Emeritus Professor of Economics
University of York
York, UK

ISBN 978-3-030-54394-5 ISBN 978-3-030-54395-2 (eBook)
https://doi.org/10.1007/978-3-030-54395-2

This Palgrave Macmillan imprint is published by the registered company Springer Nature Switzerland AG.
The registered company address is: Gewerbestrasse 11, 6330 Cham, Switzerland

To my wife, Winifred, and to our family:
Adam, Rachel, Oliver and Imogen Hartley
Professor Lucy Hartley
Dr Cecila Ellis and Martyn, Matthew Jacob, Kathryn
Olivia and Sophie Elizabeth Ellis

Preface

Much of my academic career has been devoted to defence economics. The opportunity to review and evaluate NATO after its 70 year existence was not to be missed. This book takes a non-technical economics perspective using only two diagrams! For many people NATO has been ever present: taken for granted as a well-established institution. After 70 years, it must be doing something right. This book assesses what it is doing right and what it is doing wrong.

NATO has changed massively since its formation in 1949. Who would have guessed that it would survive for 70 years and increase its membership from 12 members to 30; that it would win the Cold War; that former members of the Warsaw Pact would become NATO members; and that it would adapt to a new strategic environment, new conflicts and new technology. Despite these successes and adjustments, critics continue to question its existence. This book aims to subject myths, emotion and special pleading about NATO to economic analysis and scrutiny.

Much has been written about NATO: so why another book on the topic? The answer is that there have been few economics texts on NATO. This is a relatively short book on its economics, reviewing its achievements and challenges. It has some novel and distinctive features. First, it deals with the topical issue of burden-sharing. Second, it applies public choice analysis to NATO. Third, it explains the development of European defence policy within NATO. Fourth, it explores inefficiency in NATO and the prospects for improving its efficiency. Finally, it deals with the future challenges facing the alliance of which there are many. Throughout, economics asks searching questions about policy objectives and their costs: what are the aims of NATO and what are its costs where costs focus on the alternative uses of resources?

My first academic output on NATO was a book on *NATO Arms Co-operation: A Study in Economics and Politics* (Allen and Unwin, 1983) which resulted from a NATO Research Fellowship. Next, was a book on *The Political Economy of NATO* (with Todd Sandler, Cambridge University Press, 1999) which was written on NATO's 50th anniversary. It is fitting that this book coincides with NATO's 70th anniversary.

Many have contributed to this book, some knowingly but many unknowingly. Todd Sandler was central to developing my interests in NATO and others included Ben Solomon, Derek Braddon, David Kirkpatrick, Ron Matthews and the late Michael Intriligator and Philip Pugh. Special thanks to Ruth Jenner of Palgrave Macmillan for giving me the opportunity to write this book and to the referees who reviewed the original Proposal and commented on the final version of the book. I remain responsible for its contents.

The greatest contribution has come from my wife who has tolerated my obsession with defence economics, as well as fly fishing, football and Leeds United. My children have preferred to pursue careers in Law, English and Human Resources rather than Economics: one is much richer as a result!

York, UK Keith Hartley

Contents

List of Tables

CHAPTER 1

NATO at 70: Achievements

Abstract The formation of NATO after World War II and the start of the Cold War. Organisation, management and its main agencies are described together with its military forces and strategies.

Keywords Origins • Membership • Common fund • Threats

Introduction: An Era of Change

NATO or the North Atlantic Treaty Organisation was created in April 1949 and celebrated its 70th birthday in April 2019. Originally, there were 12 Member States with membership increasing to 30 members by 2020. A 70-year period has seen many changes which are outlined in this chapter. The Cold War ended (1990), the Warsaw Pact was dissolved (1991) and its former members joined NATO which was an extraordinary series of events. More followed with NATO involved in military conflicts in Bosnia (1995), Kosovo (1999), Afghanistan (2003) and Libya (2011). Throughout, NATO has remained a supporter of democracy.

A long-running disagreement between the USA and its European Allies over burden-sharing became more topical following the election of President Donald Trump (2016) who raised critical questions about whether NATO was worth retaining. His criticisms focused on the US paying for NATO, that it is obsolete and that it is militarily strong but

K. Hartley, *NATO at 70*,
https://doi.org/10.1007/978-3-030-54395-2_1

politically weak. These were not new US criticisms: previous US presidents and defense secretaries had made similar points. But, the 2016–2020 US criticisms were more serious. They coincided with changes in US foreign policy taken without consulting NATO and at a time when China had emerged as a new major world military power and the European Union was developing an independent defence and foreign policy. These events need to be placed in the context of the origins of NATO.

The Origins

By 1945, Europe had experienced two World Wars involving millions of deaths and injuries of military and civilian personnel and widespread destruction and damage of its cities, towns, villages and infrastructure. Peace in 1945 was against a background of what was perceived in the West to be a new and emerging threat in the form of the military and world power ambitions of the USSR. The Western view of the threat position before the creation of NATO involved Churchill's 1946 'iron curtain' speech, the Truman Doctrine (1947) and the Marshall Plan (1948). Churchill's 1946 speech referred to an iron curtain not as a physical wall but to political, military and ideological barriers erected by the Soviet Union after 1945 to separate the USSR and its allies from general contact with the West. The Truman Doctrine outlined US foreign policy to counter Soviet expansion (e.g. in Greece and Turkey); and the Marshall Plan provided gifts of foreign aid to Europe (European Recovery Program) to revive the economies of 17 Western and Southern European countries. Within Europe, tensions rose with the Berlin blockade (June 1948–May 1949). Later in 1961, the Berlin Wall was built which was an actual wall through the middle of Berlin.

Effectively, the Cold War started in 1947 with fears that the communist USSR wished to take over the world. There were concerns in the West that Soviet domination in Eastern Europe might be permanent and would be extended. Tensions between the USA and USSR reflected ideological differences and there were disagreements over Germany. It was against this background that NATO was created in 1949 as a military alliance providing collective defence for its Member States with political objectives of freedom and peace.[1] Its Article 5 was distinctive where an attack on one

[1] Lord Ismay, NATO's first Secretary General viewed NATO's purpose as 'to keep the Americans in, the Russians out and the Germans down' (Dannatt 2016, p. 116).

Member State was deemed to be an attack on all members, thereby providing a defence shield against foreign aggression. In 1955, Article 5 was extended to West Germany.

Some of the major events in NATOs history are summarised in Table 1.1. Two events are worthy of emphasis. First, NATO membership has increased over time rising from the original 12 Member States in 1949 to 30 members in 2020. An arms control treaty was signed between

Table 1.1 Timeline

Date	*Event*
1949	Formation of NATO with 12 states (April) agreed under Washington Treaty also known as North Atlantic Treaty
1952	Greece and Turkey join
1955	West Germany joins
1966	France withdraws from NATO military structure
1982	Spain joins
1990	NATO and Warsaw Pact sign Conventional Armed Forces in Europe Treaty German reunification and Berlin became a single city (October)
1991	START Treaty (2010–2021) reducing and limiting strategic offensive nuclear weapons signed by the USA and Soviet Union Warsaw Pact dissolved
1994	NATO offers former Warsaw Pact states limited association with Partnership for Peace programme (PfP)
1995	Campaign against Bosnia with air and ground forces and Implementation Force (Ifor)
1997	Ifor in Bosnia replaced with Stabilisation Force (Sfor)
1999	Czech Republic, Hungary and Poland join NATO Kosovo: start of NATO air strikes against Kosovo
2001	9/11 attacks against the USA. Article 5 invoked
2003	NATO control of International Security Assistance Force (ISAF) in Afghanistan: first major operation outside Europe Formation of Rapid Reaction Force for world-wide deployment (October)
2004	Seven nations join: Bulgaria; Estonia; Lithuania; Latvia; Romania; Slovakia; Slovenia EU replaces NATO in Bosnia
2009	Albania and Croatia join
2010	Agree new NATO Strategic Concept based on collective defence (Article 5), crisis management and cooperative security
2011	NATO no fly zone for Libya
2017	Montenegro joins (June). Total of 29 Member States
2019	US withdraws from Intermediate Range Nuclear Forces Treaty (INF: August)
2020	North Macedonia joins as 30th member

NATO and the Warsaw Pact states in 1990 and the Warsaw Pact was dissolved in 1991. In 1999, three former Warsaw Pact members joined NATO. Second, NATO's missions have changed from its deterrence mission during the Cold War to embrace new missions involving crisis management and conflict resolution (e.g. Bosnia; Kosovo; Afghanistan). A distinctive date was 2001 (9/11 terror attacks on the USA) when for the first time, NATO invoked Article 5 (although the USA chose not to involve NATO in the war against terror).

Since its formation in 1949, NATO has developed through five phases:

1. The Cold War era from 1949 to 1991 where the focus was on defence against the USSR;
2. The post-Cold War transformation of the 1990s with its focus on enlargement and out of area operations.
3. Post-September 11th, 2001, following the terrorist attacks on the USA and a focus on crisis management and stabilising Afghanistan.
4. 2010 and a new Strategic Concept embracing collective defence, crisis management and co-operative security.
5. Post-2014 with a renewed focus on deterring Russia.

Management of NATO

NATO has an established and tested management structure. This structure comprises the *North Atlantic Council* (NAC) which has governance authority and powers of decisions in NATO. There is an established NATO headquarters based in Brussels. Its *Military Committee* advises the NAC on military policy and strategy and comprises Member State's Chiefs of Defence. *Allied Command Operations* (ACO) is responsible for NATO operations world-wide. It is headed by the Supreme Allied Commander Europe (SACEUR). *Allied Command Transformation* (ACT) is responsible for the transformation and training of NATO forces and is headed by the Supreme Allied Commander, Transformation (SACT). There is a *Nuclear Planning Group* (NPG) which is NATO's senior agency for nuclear matters.

NATO has a number of agencies, including the NATO Standardization Office (NSO, formerly the NATO Standardization Agency). This Office is responsible for standardization and interoperability between Member States, reflected in Standardization Agreements (STANAGS: there are over

1200 such agreements in NATO). A *NATO Parliamentary Assembly* is the consultative inter-parliamentary organisation for the North Atlantic Alliance. In February 2018, it was decided to create two new Commands, namely, Joint Force Command for the Atlantic and a new support Command for logistics, reinforcement and military mobility. Also, a new Cyber Operations Centre was created at the military headquarters in SHAPE.

NATO Military Forces and the Infrastructure or Common Fund

NATO's military forces comprise agreed voluntary contributions from its Member States. Also, NATO has Rapid Deployable Corps which are high readiness headquarters which can be quickly dispatched to lead NATO troops within or beyond the territory of its Member States. However, NATO does own some limited common military capabilities, such as AWACS early warning radar aircraft, strategic transport aircraft and an Alliance Ground Surveillance System (AGS).

The 16 NATO AWACS aircraft are based in Germany and funded by 16 Member States. The UK contributes 'in-kind' by providing its force of AWACS to NATO. There is also a small NATO force of C-17 strategic airlifters, based in Hungary, and operated by 10 NATO allies and two Partnership for Peace nations. Additionally, the AGS comprises a NATO force of five Global Hawks (based in Italy) acquired by 15 NATO nations with operating costs shared between 26 NATO nations. AGS contributes to NATO's Joint Intelligence, Surveillance and Reconnaissance capability (JISR). These jointly owned forces illustrate the economics of clubs and partnering. Groups of members by combining their demands can achieve economies of scale in acquisition and operations so reducing costs and delivering interoperability. Such jointly owned NATO forces are different from NATO approved collaborative projects. For example, eight NATO nations are involved in a NATO multi-national project to acquire air-ground precision guided munitions which will be owned by the purchasing nations.

The costs of running NATO are borne collectively through its infrastructure or common fund. All 30 Member States contribute to the common fund using a cost-sharing formula based on gross national income. Common funding is used to finance NATO's principal budgets, namely, its civil budget (NATO HQ running costs), the military budget (costs of the integrated Command) and the NATO Security Investment Programme (military capabilities). The major contributors to the common fund for 2021 to 2024 will be the USA (16.4%), Germany (16.4%), the UK (11.3%), France (10.5%), Canada (6.9%), Spain (5.9%) and Turkey (4.7%: NATO 2019: see Table 3.5).

Military Threats to NATO

During the Cold War, the USSR was perceived to have a numerical superiority in conventional forces over the USA and NATO in Europe. In the 1950s, the USSR was seen as superior in numbers of military personnel with the Warsaw Pact having a 10:1 superiority in standing divisions. It also had considerably greater numbers of tanks and combat aircraft. But there were problems with using the conventional balance figures. They used a simple 'bean count' of numbers and there was no assessment of the quality of each nation's armed forces (e.g. training; readiness; leadership; different sizes of divisions). There was also an incentive for US and NATO forces to exaggerate and over-estimate the size of Warsaw Pact forces. Such over-estimates could be used to justify increased defence spending for NATO forces. There were similar incentives for the Warsaw Pact forces. Furthermore, a focus on the conventional balance failed to allow for the West's lead in strategic and tactical nuclear forces as well as numbers of strategic bombers.

The early 1960s and the Kennedy administration led to changes and a more balanced approach, shifting away from nuclear retaliation to a new NATO defence policy of *flexible response*. This policy relied initially on conventional forces to halt or slow USSR and Warsaw Pact attacks to avoid the early resort to the use of nuclear weapons. The Kennedy era also found that the Warsaw Pact threat was much more modest than previously believed: Warsaw Pact divisions were smaller than previously estimated and not ready for conflict. It was concluded that the West had over-estimated the size and quality of Warsaw Pact ground forces.

By the mid-to late 1960s the military gap was estimated at about 160 Soviet divisions against some 60 NATO divisions; a 3:1 Soviet advantage in tanks; and a 2:1 advantage in tactical aircraft. By 1975, the military gap remained with a USSR/Warsaw Pact force of 19,000 tanks and 4000 tactical aircraft against a US/NATO force of 7000 tanks and 2100 tactical aircraft. However, qualitatively, NATO conventional forces were superior to those of the Warsaw Pact. Soviet divisions were estimated to be one-third as effective as their US counterparts (Bitzinger 1989).

By 2020, Russia was viewed as a re-emerging major threat to both the USA and NATO, with an expanding Russian weapons programme, modernisation and expansion of its armed forces and the modernisation of its defence industrial base. New Russian weapons programmes included the development of hypersonic nuclear-capable missiles, precision strike weapons, combat robotics, supercomputing, artificial intelligence and a new generation of intermediate range ground-launched cruise missiles (which violated the INF Treaty with the US withdrawing from the Treaty).[2] The Russian threat also involved non-military measures including cyber attacks and disrupting elections in foreign states, as well as limited military actions (e.g. Syria). The Russian military threat was further reflected in the annexation of Crimea (February–March 2014) and the invasion of east Ukraine (2014–2020 continuing). From a Russian perspective, NATO was also viewed as a threat through its enlargement programme with NATO borders being shifted eastwards closer to Russia.

Russia is not the only threat to NATO. Other threats outside of Europe include China which continues to modernise its military and North Korea which forms a further threat. NATO has not only responded to threats through its defence spending but also through active military operations.

NATO Military Operations

During the Cold War, East-West tensions varied and periodically conflict threatened. Examples included the Berlin blockade of 1948–1949, the Korean War of 1950–1953 which was fought in the Far East, the construction of the Berlin Wall (1961) and the Cuban Missile Crisis of 1962. The Cold War was characterised by threats of massive nuclear retaliation and Mutually Assured Destruction (MAD) followed by the NATO doctrine of 'flexible response.'

NATO was not involved in any military operations during the Cold War. This changed with the end of the Cold War which was soon followed by a new conflict in Bosnia and Herzegovina with NATO intervening in the conflict over the period 1992 to 2004. NATO intervention to assist the United Nations peace-making forces aimed to establish long-term

[2] In 2020, it was reported that the USA was planning to withdraw from the Open Skies Treaty.

peace during and after the Bosnian War. Next, in 1999, NATO intervened in the Kosovo conflict with air strikes followed by the deployment of NATO ground forces.

A major military operation occurred following the 9/11 terror attacks on the USA which led to NATO declaring these as an Article 5 attack; but the USA did not involve NATO in the US-led military campaign which followed. Next, chronologically was April 2002 when NATO took command of the International Security Assistance Force (ISAF) in Afghanistan which was its first major operation outside Europe. In August 2004, NATO formed a training mission in Iraq which ended in December 2011. The ISAF mission ended in December 2014, to be replaced by a training mission known as the Resolute Support Mission. In the meantime, in August 2009, NATO deployed warships in the Gulf of Aden and the Indian Ocean as part of an anti-piracy operation. And in March 2011, NATO enforced an arms embargo and a *no-fly zone against Libya*, but there were disputes between members as to whether this operation was within NATO's mandate.

The Survival of NATO: Its Achievements and Challenges

The end of the Cold War in December 1989 changed the world geopolitical environment and situation. The Cold War threats ended or diminished and NATO had a challenge: was it relevant to a post-Cold War environment? What, if at all, was its role with the end of the Cold War? NATO could claim to have won the Cold War: but did it have a role for the future after 1990? Surprisingly against such a background, NATO survived, developed new missions and expanded (enlargement).

Since the end of the Cold War, NATO has achieved much. It has survived to become the most successful and powerful military alliance in history. It protected its citizens and won the Cold War without military action. Article 5 remained a key component of NATO's deterrence: it has only been used once. NATO more than doubled its membership; it created new battle groups; and its members agreed to increase their defence spending to 2% of their GDP and to spend at least 20% of their defence budget on new equipment and on defence R&D. Overall, NATO has demonstrated its ability to adapt to change, but past success does not guarantee future survival.

References

Bitzinger, R. (1989, May). *Assessing the Conventional Balance in Europe, 1945–1975*. Santa Monica: Rand.

Dannatt, R. (2016). *Boots on the Ground: Britain and Her Army since 1945*. London: Profile Books.

NATO. (2019, December). *Funding NATO*. Brussels: North Atlantic Treaty Organization.

CHAPTER 2

The Need for NATO?

Abstract The need for NATO and its survival in the new world order. NATO responding to new challenges. Threats from China and Russia, burden-sharing, rising costs, European defence policy, enlargement, new roles and new partnerships.

Keywords New world order • Future threats • Challenges

Introduction: Does NATO Have a Future?

Will NATO survive the next 70 years? Much will depend on future threats, whether NATO is viewed as the most appropriate and least-cost solution to these threats and whether NATO will adjust to survive. The future is uncertain and no one can predict it accurately. Uncertainty means the emergence of new threats embracing known/knowns but the more difficult threats are the known/unknowns and especially the unknown/unknowns. Defence policy-makers have to deal with these uncertainties. They have to make judgements about the likely future threats, the form these will take and their geographical locations over a time-scale of at least 50 years. If policy-makers get it wrong, the price paid might be defeat in battle, national conquest and foreign occupation.

Views about future threats require judgements on future military forces, non-conventional military forces (e.g. guerrilla forces; terrorists

K. Hartley, *NATO at 70*,
https://doi.org/10.1007/978-3-030-54395-2_2

and their weapons) and possible developments in new technology. NATO has to respond to these new and developing threats. It has responded successfully in the past. The classic example was the end of the Cold War when there was pressure to disband NATO. Its critics claimed that its job was done and it was no longer needed. Instead, NATO showed that it was capable of adjusting to change and acquired new roles and new members, including members from the former Warsaw Pact.

A Previous Look at the Future

A previous economic study of NATO considered its future over the period 1999 to the near term and long term (Sandler and Hartley 1999). A major issue identified was the optimal membership size of NATO and the need to measure the marginal or incremental benefits and costs that new members add to the NATO alliance. New functions appear to have been added without regard for the strains they may create for the alliance. There is also scope for developing a more dynamic theory of burden-sharing to replace current static theories. The development of the European Union's defence policy required understanding of Europe's defence industrial base and its structure, conduct and performance. Further strains on the alliance will arise from costs imposed on the same small subset of NATO allies (Sandler and Hartley 1999, p. 265).

In the near term, it was forecast that NATO will consist of two approximately equal-sized allies, namely, the USA and the European Union with defence burdens shared fairly equally. One big question identified in 1999 was whether the NATO allies were prepared to move away from unanimous decision-making to allow the alliance to act quickly. Otherwise, the fear is that as NATO admits new members, it will become less decisive and so less effective. NATO will also have to address a growing list of public good concerns. Unless free riding can be confronted, it will challenge NATOs cohesion (Sandler and Hartley 1999, p. 262).

A longer-term perspective for the period 2000 to 2010 was also considered by Sandler and Hartley (Sandler and Hartley 1999, pp. 260–264). Over the longer-term, it was possible that the USA and Canada might have left NATO with a European NATO replacing the current alliance but with a US commitment to return in an emergency. The future battlefield will comprise robots and drones with casualties in the form of assets rather than people. Greater technology will require higher R&D costs in defence industries leading to higher costs with allies having to combine their R&D

efforts and combine their purchases if these weapons are to be affordable. Climate change was anticipated with growing populations placing greater demands on air, water, land and natural resources. These pressures may lead to conflicts over the property rights to disputed resources with NATO allies possibly being involved in these conflicts (Sandler and Hartley 1999, pp. 263–264).

As with all forecasts, some are accurate, some are wrong and some await a verdict. Certainly, some of the forecasts remain relevant to the future challenges facing NATO. As always, the future is uncertain: no one can predict it accurately. Today's winners are likely to be tomorrows losers.

Future Challenges

NATO faces massive future challenges and these have been assembled around the following themes:

1. *A New World Order*
   A new world order means new threats from newly emerging military powers and new technology. There has been a shift from the single threat from the former Soviet Union during the Cold War to a new world order of complex and changing threats creating a new security environment with a new range of risks and a diverse spectrum of threats. NATO is now facing threats on three strategic fronts: namely, the home, eastern and southern fronts. The result is threats which are geographically diverse requiring varying responses with individual Member States expecting NATO to respond to their specific national requirements. As a result, NATO is finding these diverse risks are unmanageable leading to strategic overload.

   China is an obvious example with questions as to whether it is within NATO's sphere of influence. The immediate China threat might involve Taiwan, the possibility of conflict and the probable involvement of the USA. An emergent Russia, cyber warfare, terrorism and space weapons form additional threats. In future, the USA will focus on the threats from China and Russia. Further new threats are likely to involve interference in national elections, the exploitation of organised crime networks, online intervention and infrastructure attacks (trains; hospitals, utilities; IT networks). For the future, the USA prefers Europe to be militarily self-sufficient and responsible for its own defence and to contribute to the defence of the Middle East and North Africa. Instead, there are US concerns that NATO Europe is 'facing death by a thousand cuts' as European members fail to increase their military spending and achieve the NATO target of spending 2% of their GDP on defence.

The new threats have been summarised: the end of the Cold War has resulted in the slaying of a large dragon to be replaced by life in a jungle filled with a bewildering variety of poisonous snakes (Kilcullen 2020). Threats and enemies have evolved in a Darwinian fashion. After the Gulf War, terrorists concluded that it was madness to engage the West militarily on its own terms. Each generation of the West's foes is learning new lessons (e.g. about monitoring communications to avoid detection). There is also a view that the long years of Western air superiority are ending with a future of unjammable cheap drones operated by non-state adversaries able to deploy swarms of flying killers. Critics of NATO ask why it continues to buy costly weapons systems such as F-35s when Ikea-type platforms are perfectly adequate (Hastings 2020)?

Threats have emerged in new forms. The Chinese and Russians are using methods designed to cause chaos but just short of provoking a western military response. Examples include militias, surrogates, cyber attacks, fake news and 'little green men' (non-uniformed Russian personnel) Also, overt and violent conflict is a small component of conflict: non-military measures might dominate any confrontation (Hastings 2020; Kilcullen 2020).

2. *Threats from within NATO*

There are internal threats from within Member States. For example, voters in European states have a preference for social welfare spending rather than defence spending leading to charges of 'lethargy' in NATO with continued peace resulting in complacency. Similarly, the USA is increasingly reluctant to continue 'paying for European defence' which is seen as militarily weak in airlift, air tankers, intelligence, surveillance and drones. Members are also concerned about the position of Turkey as a reliable ally reflected in its preference for a Russian missile defence system and its involvement in the Syrian conflict (e.g. Idlib).

There is a more general problem of securing support for defence within democracies. Often, political leaders fail to explain threats to voters, apart from the obvious one from terrorism. The result is that voters become indifferent to national security issues.

3. *Burden-sharing*
   The continuing debate between the USA and Europe over burden-sharing. The USA claims that it is bearing an unfair share of NATO's defence burden although such a claim is sensitive to definitions and the identity and views of the US President. For example, President Trump has been critical of NATO and Europe's limited defence contribution (see Chap. 3). One view claims that President Trump values "unpredictability, decision by impulse, sowing discord among allies and thereby spreading deep uncertainty. But in such an atmosphere, if posturing and power games go wrong ... conflict might become a calculated risk" (Spohr 2019, p. 74).
4. *Costs*
   Defence equipment is costly and unit costs in real terms continue to increase. The long-term trend forecasts a single ship navy, a single tank army and Starship Enterprise for the air force. The future is likely to be one of smaller Armed Forces, fewer new projects and shorter production runs for national defence industries.
5. *Migration*
   International and illegal migration is especially affecting the southern NATO countries (e.g. Greece, Greek Islands, Turkey). Large movements of peoples are creating pressure on local populations and local resources. As a result, tensions arise within NATO and the EU over the desirable allocation of refugee populations. Which European nations are willing to accept and pay for migrant labour is another aspect of burden-sharing.

   There is another dimension which is affecting US attitudes towards NATO. Increasingly, the US population comprises more non-European immigrants leading to less support and willingness for the USA to be involved in the European dimension of NATO.
6. *Trust*
   Loss of trust between Member States. Turkey is an example of a nation which has established links with Russia involving the purchase of the Russian S400 missile defence system. Also, Turkey is involved in Syria and conflict with the Kurds in Syria, leading to speculation about Turkey's possible exit from NATO.

7. *European defence policy*
   European efforts to create an independent and strategically autonomous defence industry, an independent defence policy and an independent European army might be a future threat to NATO.

   The European Union has launched a number of defence initiatives including the 2016 European Defence Action Plan (EDAP), a European Defence Fund, Permanent Structured Cooperation (PESCO) and the European Intervention Initiative. The challenge for NATO is to integrate these various EU defence initiatives into NATO and a new transatlantic initiative between the USA and the EU *within* NATO (see Chap. 5). But the EU has its problems: its institutions are unable to function effectively with 27 different members each with different visions of their future. Also, the EU has failed to develop as a serious foreign policy actor so that the onus to act and enforce peace returned to the USA and NATO which had to adapt its doctrine to 'out-of-area' missions (Spohr 2019, p. 74).
8. *New members: Enlargement*
   Questions arise as to whether there is a limit to the size of NATO and if so, what is this limit? Is NATO 'too large' and what about possible new members from Sweden, Finland, Georgia and Ukraine? Each new member raises issues about their costs and benefits. There are fears that the eastward expansion of NATO will be viewed as a threat to Russia.
9. *New roles*
   New roles are emerging for NATO and its geographical sphere of influence. Should it have a role in space; should there be a greater focus on special forces and maritime forces rather than large-scale land forces; and ballistic missile defence for the Member States? New technology means new threats from cyber warfare, artificial intelligence, space, robots and UAVs. Critics regard NATO as strategically 'brain dead' and no longer relevant to 2020 and beyond.
10. *Decision-making*
    With the increase in its size, NATO needs a new decision-making organisation capable of making speedy decisions responding quickly to a range of new threats. More members mean that decision-making will be slower when reality requires speedier decision-making. The larger organisation cannot be embedded in slow procedures requiring unanimity from large numbers of members.

11. *The NATO social contract*
    There are fears about the end of the traditional social contract underpinning NATO. Under the traditional contract, the USA bore Europe's defence burden with Europe accepting and supporting US foreign policy. The new world order requires a new NATO social contract. What role will NATO play in the new global power struggle?
12. *Threats below Article 5*
    NATO needs to consider whether it should respond to threats which are below the Article 5 threshold (at the sub-Article 5 level). An example was the UK Salisbury Russian-sponsored chemical attacks and the response of some NATO members through the expulsion of Russian diplomats.
13. *New partnerships*
    There is scope for NATO expanding and creating new partnerships for peace with other countries. Which nations are potential candidates for new partnerships with NATO?
14. *Brexit*
    The UK exited the EU in January 2020 but remains a member of NATO. The UK's precise role in European defence post-Brexit remains to be resolved: the UK's military role will affect its contribution to European defence within NATO.
15. *Pandemics*
    The 2020 coronavirus pandemic poses a threat to world health including the health of citizens of Member States. The pandemic involves transnational externalities where actions in one country create benefits and/or costs in other nations. The pandemic is mainly a medical and health problem with no immediately obvious military aspects which might involve NATO. However, NATO has a role in providing international collective military action. It can provide additional resources to national governments in such forms as military personnel, transport, communications, accommodation and medical treatment for sick patients. For example, national governments might need transport for delivering food and medical supplies to vulnerable citizens; they might need additional military personnel and surveillance systems to protect national borders, so reducing the international transmission of the virus. Increased border protection might also be needed to control illegal immigration which might be a further source of interna-

tional virus transmission. In these forms, NATO provides club goods which are available to Member States only. Pandemics have a further dimension in that they can be used in cyber warfare to create disinformation by potential adversaries (e.g. Russia; China) leading to loss of trust between allies. Pandemics also remind us of the potential threats from biological weapons. Higher public spending on health care emergencies might require compensatory reductions in other government spending with national defence spending a candidate for cuts.

NATO has survived by adapting to change. It has changed its traditional focus on collective defence to include out-of-area crisis management missions, cooperative security partnerships with non-NATO partners across the globe, training and advisory efforts in Africa and the Middle East and strategies to manage and respond to threats which are below the level of armed conflict (sub-Article 5 level). NATO must build on its strengths which include its established and integrated command structure, its force generation capability, interoperability standards and other political and military decision-making structures (Ellehuus 2019).

One view on NATO's future is that its biggest challenge will be to prevent separation (divorce) between the USA and Europe. The obvious question is whether Europe is a burden on the Americans and whether European weakness makes America weaker? Burden-sharing will continue to be a major issue within NATO. Economics can contribute to understanding of this issue and many others in the list of challenges facing NATO. Other challenges include enlargement, European defence policy, trust, new roles and decision-making. But the issue of burden-sharing dominates the immediate future.

References

Ellehuus, R. (2019). *NATO at 70—Shaping the Future for the Next 70 Years*. Washington, DC: Commentary by Center for Strategic and International Studies.

Hastings, M. (2020, March 8). The West v the Rest, Book Review by Max Hastings. *The Times*, pp. 35.

Kilcullen, D. (2020). *Dragons and the Snakes: How the Rest Learned to Fight the West*. London: Hurst.

Sandler, T., & Hartley, K. (1999). *The Political Economy of NATO*. Cambridge: Cambridge University Press.
Spohr, K. (2019). 1989–2019: How the End of the Cold War Shaped Today's World, An Interview with Kristina Spohr. *RUSI Journal, 164*(7), 68–76.

CHAPTER 3

Burden-Sharing

Abstract The burden-sharing debate is analysed using economic models and supporting data. Various burden-sharing measures are reviewed and stress is placed on defence outputs rather than inputs. The Olson-Zeckhauser model is described, then the joint products model and the concept of force thinning.

Keywords Public goods • Flexible response • Exploitation hypothesis • The 2% target

Introduction: The Policy Issues

NATO is the world's oldest and most successful military alliance but at age 70, it remains controversial. The USA continues to be critical of the defence contribution of its allies, claiming that America bears an unfair burden with threats to withdraw from the Alliance. US concerns about defence burdens in NATO are not new. President Trump is the latest in a list of US presidents and defense secretaries who have criticised the inadequate European defence effort, especially that of Germany. Europe has been criticised for failing to invest more in its security and for ignoring the US requests. Some US critics have been more precise suggesting that NATO lacks a range of military assets (e.g. helicopters; transport aircraft; maintenance, intelligence, surveillance capabilities).

K. Hartley, *NATO at 70*,
https://doi.org/10.1007/978-3-030-54395-2_3

Following the burden-sharing debates, Member States have agreed to two new NATO spending targets. First, a commitment to spend at least 2% of their GDP on defence (the 2% commitment which is the most widely known). Second, a commitment to spend 20% of their defence budgets on the development and acquisition of equipment (the equipment commitment). Since 2006, only eight countries have achieved both targets simultaneously, namely, Bulgaria, France, Greece, Latvia, Poland, Turkey, the UK and the USA.

Critics claim that with the end of the Cold War, NATO is no longer needed. Nor is there a need for increased NATO defence spending with critics claiming that the funds would be better used on health and social care spending. This raises a more general concern as to whether there are genuine threats facing NATO which justify its continued existence. Does NATO have a future or should it be disbanded? Or, will pressure from the European Union to create an alternative EU Defence Force lead to Europe withdrawing from NATO?

This chapter focuses on the burden-sharing debate. It reviews various measures of defence burdens; it includes a critique of burden-sharing; and it relates burden-sharing to economic models of alliances.

Statistical Overview

What is known, what is not known and what needs to be known to assess NATOs defence effort and burdens? Much is known; much is not known; and much needs to be known. Some of what is known is shown in Tables 3.1 and 3.2. These show for each NATO nation total defence spending and numbers of military personnel over the period 2012–2019.

The USA dominates the list of nations by total defence spending. In 2019, it accounted for about 70% of total NATO defence spending, with NATO Europe accounting for some 28% of the NATO total. The UK was the second largest defence spender, accounting for some 7% of total NATO defence spending, followed by France and Germany. Using the levels of defence spending, the smallest contributors were Estonia, Slovenia, Luxembourg, Albania and Montenegro. In terms of real increases in defence spending between 2012 and 2019, NATO Europe increased defence spending by +16% compared with a real terms reduction of −8% by the USA (see Table 3.1). Comparing defence spending in 2012 and 2019, the country rankings showed little change: small changes occurred for the nations with relatively low defence spending.

Table 3.1 NATO defence expenditure 2012–2019 million US dollars, constant 2015 prices

Nation	*2012*	*2019*
NATO Europe	*239,924*	*277,858*
Albania	161 (27)	166 (27)
Belgium	4586 (13)	4494 (13)
Bulgaria	635 (21)	927 (22)
Croatia	744 (20)	970 (20)
Czech Republic	1829 (17)	2513 (17)
Denmark	3898 (14)	4434 (14)
Estonia	406 (23)	569 (24)
France	44,460 (3)	47,705 (4)
Germany	42,443 (4)	49,132 (3)
Greece	4632 (12)	4624 (12)
Hungary	1156 (18)	1739 (19)
Italy	24,273 (5)	23,281 (5)
Latvia	221 (25)	622 (23)
Lithuania	287 (24)	933 (21)
Luxembourg	193 (26)	345 (26)
Montenegro	62 (28)	78 (28)
Netherlands	9178 (9)	11,360 (10)
Norway	5580 (11)	7014 (11)
Poland	7643 (10)	11,376 (9)
Portugal	2759 (15)	3064 (16)
Romania	1962 (16)	4368 (15)
Slovak Republic	882 (19)	1754 (18)
Slovenia	485 (22)	525 (25)
Spain	12,089 (7)	12,336 (8)
Turkey	11,294 (8)	18,000 (7)
UK	58,129 (2)	65,527 (2)
North America	*757,116*	*706,376*
Canada	16,053 (6)	21,277 (6)
USA	741,064 (1)	685,099 (1)
NATO TOTAL	*997,040*	*984,234*

Source: NATO (2019b)

Notes: (i) Defence expenditure does not include pensions; (ii) data are in million US dollars at constant 2015 prices and exchange rates. Figures for 2019 are estimates; (iii) figures in brackets show rankings for each year

Table 3.2 NATO military personnel thousands

Country	*2012*	*2019*
NATO Europe	*1956*	*1849*
Albania	7.9	6.8
Belgium	31	26
Bulgaria	26	25
Croatia	16	15
Czech Republic	22	26
Denmark	19	17
Estonia	6.0	6.3
France	219	208
Germany	192	184
Greece	110	105
Hungary	19	20
Italy	189	179
Latvia	4.7	6.4
Lithuania	8.3	15.9
Luxembourg	0.8	0.9
Montenegro	1.9	1.6
Netherlands	44	41
Norway	21	20
Poland	98	123
Portugal	34	30
Romania	66	69
Slovak Republic	13	13
Slovenia	7.1	6.8
Spain	125	121
Turkey	495	435
UK	184	144
North America	*1467*	*1410*
Canada	68	72
USA	1400	1338
NATO Total	*3423*	*3258*

Source: NATO (2019b)

The list of NATO defence spenders in 2019 can be divided into five groups (Table 3.1):

1. The leading spender, namely, the USA.
2. The next top defence spenders with annual spending ranging from $48 billion to $66 billion: UK, Germany and France.

3. Middle-level defence spenders with spending ranging from $7 billion to $25 billion: Italy, Canada, Turkey, Spain, Norway, Netherlands and Poland.
4. Low-level defence spending nations with spending ranging from $1 billion to $5 billion: Belgium, Czech Republic, Denmark, Greece, Hungary, Portugal, Romania and the Slovak Republic.
5. The rest with annual spending of under $1 billion: Albania, Bulgaria, Croatia, Estonia, Latvia, Lithuania, Luxembourg, Montenegro and Slovenia. Montenegro ranked bottom in 2019 with annual military spending of $78 million (2015 prices). This group raises the question of why NATO agreed to their membership: they involved collective defence commitments by all other members of the Alliance in return for nominal contributions to collective NATO defence.

Numbers of military personnel are a further indicator of burden-sharing. Table 3.2 shows the relative scale of the difference in burden-sharing between the USA and its allies based on numbers of military personnel. In 2019, the USA contributed over 40% of the total number of NATO military personnel. Next was Turkey contributing some 13% of total NATO military personnel, followed by France (6%), Germany (5.6%), Italy (5.5%) and the UK (4.4%). Over the period 2012 to 2019, most members reduced their numbers of military personnel (exceptions included Canada; Poland; and the Czech Republic). The smallest military personnel contributions were from Luxembourg and Montenegro contributing 900 and 1600 military personnel, respectively.

Typically, defence shares of GDP are used to measure a nation's defence burden as shown in Table 3.3. Two points emerge from this table. First, the USA bears the highest defence burden with a share of 3.42% of GDP in 2019. This compares with a 2019 defence share of 1.58% for NATO Europe. Second, the table identifies those nations spending 2% or more of their GDP on defence: NATO nations have agreed a target to spend 2% of their GDP on defence. Only six European nations achieved this target in 2019. These were Estonia, Greece, Latvia, Poland, Romania and the UK. The nations failing to achieve the 2% target included France, Germany, Italy, the Netherlands and Canada.

At first sight, the data on defence shares support the US claim that it is bearing the burden of NATO defence spending and that Europe is free riding. Amongst the larger nations, Germany has an especially low defence share (1.36%). However, simple share figures can be misleading as burden

Table 3.3 Burden-sharing in NATO, 2012–2019, 2015 prices and exchange rates

Nation	*Defence share of GDP 2012 (%)*	*Defence share of GDP 2019 (%)*	*GDP per capita 2019 (US$ 000s)*
NATO Europe	*1.55*	*1.58*	*30.6*
Albania	1.49	1.26	4.6
Belgium	1.04	0.93	42.1
Bulgaria	1.34	1.61	8.2
Croatia	1.53	1.75	13.6
Czech Republic	1.05	1.19	19.8
Denmark	1.35	1.35	56.2
Estonia	1.90	2.13	20.1
France	1.87	1.84	38.6
Germany	1.31	1.36	43.4
Greece	2.29	2.24	19.3
Hungary	1.03	1.21	14.7
Italy	1.32	1.22	31.4
Latvia	0.88	2.01	16.2
Lithuania	0.76	1.98	16.9
Luxembourg	0.38	0.55	99.7
Montenegro	1.66	1.65	7.6
Netherlands	1.24	1.35	48.4
Norway	1.52	1.70	76.8
Poland	1.74	2.01	14.7
Portugal	1.41	1.41	21.2
Romania	1.23	2.04	11.0
Slovak Republic	1.09	1.74	18.4
Slovenia	1.17	1.04	24.3
Spain	1.04	0.92	28.5
Turkey	1.59	1.89	11.7
UK	2.16	2.13	46.0
North America	*4.11*	*3.26*	*58.9*
Canada	1.09	*1.27*	44.7
USA	4.37	3.42	60.5
NATO TOTAL	*2.94*	*2.51*	*41.6*

Source: NATO (2019b)

Notes: (i) Figures are for defence spending as a percentage share of GDP (%) based on 2015 prices and exchange rates; (ii) defence expenditure does not include pensions; (iii) at time of publication, the 2019 figures were estimates; (iv) Iceland is a member of NATO but has no standing army and no armed forces. The published NATO figures do not show any defence spending for Iceland. An internet search showed Iceland's defence share of GDP at 0.1% in 2012 and 0.26% in 2015 indicators. For example, the US share figures show total US defence spending on its *world-wide* defence activities and not solely on the defence of Europe. In contrast, most if not all European military spending is allocated to the defence of Europe. Also, other indicators such as the contribution of military forces to UN peace-keeping operations might measure an ally's contribution to international peace-keeping and might be regarded as part of its defence burden contribution within NATO. Nor should benefits be ignored. All Member States, including the USA, derive benefits from defence spending and these need to be included in an overall evaluation of both the benefits and costs of NATO membership. More significantly, the use of defence shares as a burden indicator places the focus on inputs rather than defence outputs. In the absence of a satisfactory measure of defence output, it was assumed that outputs were measured by inputs on the (incorrect) assumption that inputs equalled outputs!

Data are also available on NATO nations distribution of defence expenditure by main category comprising equipment, personnel, infrastructure and other categories (e.g. operations and maintenance spending, other R&D expenditure and expenditure not shown elsewhere). The data are percentages of each nation's total defence spending and they indicate which nations are capital-intensive (equipment) and labour-intensive (personnel) in their military forces. The data also show which Member States are achieving the NATO 20% equipment spending target (16 nations in 2019).

Unlike the other indicators of defence burdens, the USA does not dominate the different categories. Equipment accounted for 27.5% of 2019 US defence spending with personnel accounting for 39.6%, infrastructure for 1.3% and the 'other' category accounting for 32.6% of its budget. On this basis, in 2019, there were five nations which were more capital-intensive than the USA, namely, Lithuania, Luxembourg, Norway, Slovak Republic and Turkey. This shows the limitations of the measure. None of these five nations have obviously better-equipped Armed Forces than the USA with its F-22 and F-35 aircraft, stealth bombers, aircraft carriers and nuclear-powered submarines. Similarly, a substantial number of NATO nations had more labour-intensive forces than the USA; but personnel share figures fail to show the *numbers* of personnel and their *quality* as reflected in human capital inputs (e.g. training: see Table 3.4).

Table 3.4 Defence expenditure by category, 2019, percentage of total defence expenditure (%)

Nation	*Equipment*	*Personnel*	*Infrastructure*	*Other*
Albania	14.4	64.8	2.0	18.8
Belgium	10.8	68.7	1.3	19.3
Bulgaria	25.1	56.2	0.6	18.1
Canada	11.3	49.7	3.4	35.6
Croatia	11.6	68.5	2.3	17.6
Czech Republic	14.5	(54.6)	(5.4)	(29.4)
Denmark	17.0	(49.9)	(1.5)	(37.0)
Estonia	19.4	34.3	5.6	40.7
France	24.4	(46.9)	(3.5)	(25.9)
Germany	16.4	(47.0)	(3.9)	(35.0)
Greece	12.5	69.6	0.1	17.8
Hungary	23.5	41.7	3.5	31.3
Italy	20.6	(65.7)	(1.9)	(11.3)
Latvia	25.3	35.3	7.6	31.8
Lithuania	28.7	43.3	5.1	22.9
Luxembourg	44.6	(32.8)	4.7	(18.5)
Montenegro	14.3	64.5	4.0	17.3
Netherlands	23.1	45.3	3.2	28.4
Norway	29.5	32.8	7.6	30.1
Poland	23.9	48.3	5.3	22.6
Portugal	11.0	(71.8)	(0.4)	(14.9)
Romania	24.8	56.9	4.6	13.7
Slovak Republic	41.7	40.6	1.9	15.8
Slovenia	8.0	(72.4)	(0.5)	(18.9)
Spain	20.7	60.8	1.1	17.4
Turkey	38.6	46.8	2.0	12.6
UK	24.1	35.6	1.9	38.4
USA	27.5	38.6	1.3	32.6

Source: NATO (2019b)

Notes: (i) Figures in brackets are for 2018 and these numbers do not total to 100%; (ii) figures are rounded

Common Infrastructure

NATO's collective or common funding finances three major areas. First, the civil budget funds NATO headquarters, its staff, committees and planning groups. Second, the military budget supports NATO military commands, its staff and committees. Third, its physical infrastructure such as pipelines, satellites, communication networks and airfields. The country distribution of these costs is shown in Table 3.5 which presents an alternative indicator of NATO burden-sharing. The infrastructure burden-shares show a different ranking compared with the ranking by defence shares of GDP. Infrastructure burdens show a much higher ranking for Germany which is similar to the USA. Low rankings are shown for Iceland, Albania,

Table 3.5 Cost share arrangements for NATO common infrastructure budget, 2021–2024

Nation	*2021–2024* *Costs shares of NATO common infrastructure budget (%)*
Albania	0.09
Belgium	2.11
Bulgaria	0.37
Canada	6.88
Croatia	0.29
Czech Republic	1.06
Denmark	1.31
Estonia	0.12
France	10.49
Germany	16.35
Greece	1.06
Hungary	0.76
Iceland	0.06
Italy	8.79
Latvia	0.16
Lithuania	0.26
Luxembourg	0.17
Netherlands	3.45
Norway	1.78
Poland	2.99
Portugal	1.05
Romania	1.23
Slovakia	0.52
Slovenia	0.23
Spain	5.99
Turkey	4.73
UK	11.29
USA	16.36
TOTAL	*100.00*

Source: NATO (2019a)

Estonia and Slovenia. Overall, the Spearman rank correlation coefficient between defence burdens for 2019 and the cost shares for 2021–2024 was +0.14 which was not significant (Tables 3.3 and 3.5).

The Burden-Sharing Debate: Inputs Versus Outputs?

NATO burden-sharing debates embrace positive and normative economics and are about *what is* and *what ought to be*. They are about the actual contribution of each Member State to collective alliance defence and the '*fairness*' of each member's contribution. Inevitably, equity issues are controversial and for NATO they require international agreement on whether Member States should contribute to the alliance on the basis of the benefits received or the ability-to-pay with payments (c.f. taxation) based on a proportional or progressive basis. In fact, members contribute to NATO through cash payments for NATO's common budgets, through payments-in-kind in the form of the allocation of national military forces to NATO command and host-nation provision of military bases and over-flying rights (Hartley and Sandler 1999). However, an ability to pay indicator exists in the form of GDP per capita. For 2019, a Spearman's rank correlation between defence shares of GDP and per capita income was negative at −0.12 which was not significant at the 5% level. An example is Turkey which ranked 9th in defence shares but 24th in per capita income whilst Luxembourg was first in per capita income but 28th in defence shares.

The burden-sharing debate requires the selection of an appropriate indicator. Here, much depends on what is being measured. The most commonly used measure of defence burdens is defence shares of national output (D/GDP); but it has its limitations. Nations can use different definitions of defence spending (e.g. pensions; police forces; defence R&D); and some countries rely on conscript forces so that their defence budgets under-estimate their defence burdens as reflected in opportunity costs. Member States also have varying mixes of public and country-specific military forces reflected in the allocation of their budgets between nuclear and conventional forces and in the geographical distribution of their conventional forces between NATO areas and overseas protection (e.g. colonies). The combat effectiveness of armed forces will differ between Member States reflected in the age or vintage of their equipment, their training inputs, combat readiness, the experience of their commanders and the battle experience of their armed forces.

Quantification has its limitations. Columns of statistics do not measure some of the qualitative benefits of an alliance. Monetary and quantitative measures do not reflect a member's commitment to NATO in the form of its willingness to support the alliance leader (e.g. willingness to provide basing and overflying rights for US forces). This can be represented by *trust* between members showing their willingness to support alliance collective military action. For example, in the event of an Article 5 intervention, will other members 'turn-up?' There are wider political and economic benefits and costs associated with a military alliance (see Chap. 5). Some of these qualitative factors can be represented by transaction costs and benefits including the 'looseness' and 'tightness' of linkages between Member States and the extent of integration. To be viable, NATO needs to provide net linkage benefits to the alliance as a whole so that every member receives a net benefit from membership.

There are alternative indicators of burden-sharing some of which provide different rankings of burden-sharing. These include:

1. *Numbers of military personnel and their geographical location.* Table 3.6 shows the numbers of US military personnel based in Europe and the rest of the world. There were almost 200,000 US military personnel based overseas with some 32% based in Europe

Table 3.6 Overseas US military forces, 2019

Country	*US numbers*
Europe	
Germany	35,275 (178,600)
Italy	12,902 (174,500)
UK	9254 (146,500)
Spain	3525 (121,200)
Total Europe	*63,709*
Rest of World	
Japan	57,094
Hawaii	42,386
South Korea	26,643
Total SE Asia	*133,449*

Source: World Population Review, 17th February, 2020

Notes: (i) Numbers are for December 2019; (ii) figures in brackets show numbers of active military personnel for each nation shown: For example 178,600 personnel for Germany. In July 2020, the USA announced the withdrawal of almost 12,000 troops from Germany with some 6400 troops returning to the USA and 5600 to other European countries (e.g. Italy, Poland)

and almost 70% based in the rest of the world. In late 2019, most of the US military personnel based in Europe were air force and army personnel, comprising 27,774 Air Force personnel, 25,808 Army personnel and 7829 Navy personnel. Overall, the US numbers in Europe represented some 5% of total US military personnel. The numbers of US military personnel deployed in Europe are also much smaller than the numbers of national forces based in each European nation. For example, there were almost 35,000 US military personnel based in Germany compared with nearly 180,000 German military personnel based in Germany. On this basis, the European nations appear to be bearing a larger burden than the USA for the defence of Europe; but, of course, the USA will claim that its total numbers of military personnel are the relevant figure measuring total military capability.

2. *Equipment measures.* Using equipment shares of defence budgets, Luxembourg was ranked first whilst the USA was ranked sixth in NATO in 2019. But, simple share figures do not reflect the quality of equipment inputs.
3. *Arms trade* data showing the balance of arms exports and imports within NATO might be used as an alternative indicator of burden-sharing. However, since international trade is voluntary and mutually-beneficial for traders, it is far from clear that it is a burden. Instead, this indicator might be an example of special pleading with European members of NATO demonstrating that they are net purchasers of US arms which they claim needs to be included in any overall assessment of burden-sharing. For the period 2018–2019, arms imports by NATO Europe accounted for 16% of total US arms exports with the USA achieving a balance of trade surplus on its arms trade with NATO Europe (a trade surplus of $2.2 billion for 2018–2019).[1] The major NATO Europe arms importers from the USA were Norway, the Netherlands, Italy, the UK and Turkey.
4. *Other burden-sharing indicators are available* such as defence R&D, peacekeeping expenditure and payments of overseas aid. Again, different indicators can give different country rankings. However, whilst different defence burden measures are available, the behaviour of alternative measures over time has given consistent results, so

[1] Data based on SIPRI Trend Indicator Values (TIVs) which measure the volume of arms transfers and not the value of transfers.

making it less important which indicator is used (Sandler and Hartley 1999, p. 46). However, a more recent study of European Armed Force's burden-sharing behaviour found that the selection of specific performance measures made a difference to a country's rankings. For example, depending on the choice of indicator, Austria was ranked between 8th and 19th and Greece between 1st and 18th (Beeres and Bogers 2012).

Future Burden-Sharing Debates?

NATO burden-sharing debates have been dominated by myths, half-truths, emotion and special pleading. Self-interest dictates that each nation will use the burden-sharing indicator which shows that it is bearing its 'fair' share or an 'unfairly' high share of the alliance defence effort. Problems arise since there is no agreed single comprehensive measure of each nation's contribution to the alliance defence effort where contributions are multi-product and multi-dimensional. In the absence of agreement about the best indicator, nations will continue to rely on using defence shares of GDP as their best and preferred indicator. One way forward would be an agreement between Member States to study alternative indicators and select one or a few as possible solutions. Predictably, when such a study presents a range of alternatives, the pact leader will favour the indicator which shows it bearing a large burden.

Economic Models of Military Alliances

Surprisingly, economists have contributed to the understanding of many of the issues affecting the future of NATO starting with the development of economic theories of military alliances. It is surprising because a military alliance is not within the traditional scope of economics: it is more appropriate for politics, international relations and strategic studies. An economic theory of a military alliance has to explain the existence of the alliance, burden-sharing, enlargement and the optimal size of the club. The economic model has developed from the economics of collective action, the theory of clubs, public and club goods and transaction cost economics.

NATO can be viewed as a voluntary international club which specialises in providing collective defence in the form of a public good. In this respect it has some resemblance to other clubs such as those for angling, golf and tennis. Individuals and nations join clubs and remain members so long as membership is worthwhile in the form of expected benefits exceeding costs. As a result, NATO survives so long as it offers more protection and security and/or lower defence costs compared with national independence (i.e. non-membership). Membership benefits take the form of collective defence including the protection offered by the US strategic nuclear umbrella and the protection from Article 5 where an attack on one member is regarded as an attack on all members. The costs of membership include a contribution to NATO's common infrastructure (e.g. airfields; communications; pipelines), the commitment of national military forces to NATO, the provision of bases to other members and a willingness to accept the rules of the club.

Economists recognise a specific class of goods known as club goods which are a sub-category of public goods that are excludable but non-rivalrous.[2] Excludability arises since the club can exclude non-members who have not paid the entrance fee. The non-rival feature of club goods arises since additional consumption of defence is not at the expense of anyone else's consumption of defence which makes it a non-rivalrous good. All club members can access the club good up to the point of congestion or full capacity. Public goods take the club model further.

NATO is an example of a military alliance offering a public good in the form of collective defence. It emerged and survived because it was a worthwhile organisation offering benefits which greatly exceeded its costs.[3] The original model of military alliances was based on the provision of nuclear deterrence as a pure public good and provided some significant hypotheses. First, defence burdens are expected to be shared unevenly between allies: large wealthy allies bear the defence burden for the smaller and poorer allies. Unequal burden sharing results in free-riding behaviour where some nations rely for their defence on the military efforts of their

[2] Public goods have two features, namely, non-rivalry and non-excludability. Non-rivalry means that my consumption of defence does not affect other people's consumption of defence and non-excludability means that once provided no individual can exclude others from the consumption of defence. In contrast, club goods are excludable but non-rivalrous. Private goods are both excludable and rivalrous.

[3] The original pioneering work on the economics of military alliances was undertaken by Mancur Olson (1965) and later by Olson and Zeckhauser (1966). Olson's book on The Logic of Collective Action rests on a single premise, namely, that individual rationality is not sufficient for collective rationality (Sandler 1992).

allies (e.g. Canada relying on the USA). This became known as the *exploitation hypothesis.* A second hypothesis predicts that the more defence is provided by a nation's allies, the less that nation spends on defence. A third hypothesis predicts that there is no need to limit the size of an alliance since the addition of an ally adds positive net marginal benefits as costs are shared between a large number of members but benefits are not diminished for existing allies. Creating or joining an alliance means that its members achieve more military security and lower defence costs than they had before joining the alliance. A fourth hypothesis modifies the conventional demand for military expenditure model by including an alliance variable. It states that an ally's demand for defence depends on the ally's income, the level of its allies' defence spending as well as relative prices and the perceived threat (Hartley 2011, p. 73).

Evidence supported the exploitation hypothesis, namely, that the larger a nation, the higher its valuation of the output of an alliance. This hypothesis was tested using data for 1964 and it was found that there was a significant positive correlation between the size of a member's national income and its share of national income spent on defence (Olson and Zeckhauser 1966, p. 289).

A limitation of the original 1966 Olson and Zeckhauser model of military alliances was its assumption that the costs of defence were constant to scale and the same for all alliance members. This assumption is unrealistic and it is unlikely that costs are constant and uniform. Instead, it is more likely that defence industries are decreasing cost industries and that costs differ between Member States reflecting different comparative advantages.

The model also has implications for the current US criticism of NATO. It shows that the advantage usually rests with the smaller nations for two reasons. First, the large country (e.g. USA) "loses more from withholding an alliance contribution than a small country does, since it values a given amount of alliance force more highly. Second, the large country has relatively less to gain than its small ally from driving a hard bargain" (Olson and Zeckhauser 1966, p. 289). Other studies provided further support for the exploitation hypothesis (Sandler and Hartley 2001, p. 883). Additional evidence seemed to support the advantage resting with the smaller nations. In 2019, the USA accounted for 70% of NATO defence spending whilst the next largest allies, namely, France, Germany and the UK, each accounted for some 5–7% of NATO defence spending. Similarly, in 2019, defence burdens shown by defence as a share of GDP differed between the USA at 3.4% of GDP and NATO Europe at some

1.6% of GDP (see Table 3.3). Even in 1966, Olson and Zeckhauser concluded that "American attempts to persuade other nations to bear "fair" shares of the burdens of common ventures are likely to be divisive and harmful even to American interest in the long run" (Olson and Zeckhauser 1966, p. 293).

The next development in the economics of alliances was the *joint product model.* This allowed defence to provide a variety of defence outputs on a spectrum between purely public, purely private and impurely public between allies. On this basis, alliance defence output provides deterrence, protection or damage limitation and private or national-specific benefits. Strategic nuclear forces provide more purely public benefits in the form of deterrence and are not subject to force thinning. In contrast, conventional forces are prone to force thinning as they are spread out to defend an exposed border. Increasing the concentration of troops and weapons along one ally's border might make another ally's border more vulnerable. Conventional forces have further features. Unlike strategic nuclear forces, they can be deployed for country-specific benefits such as controlling civil unrest, responding to terrorism and providing humanitarian and disaster relief.

Strategic doctrine and weapons technology can affect the mix of joint products. For the period 1949 to 1966, NATO's strategic doctrine relied on *nuclear deterrence in the form of mutually assured destruction (MAD)*: any Soviet expansion at the expense of NATO members would lead to massive nuclear response by the USA, France and Britain. Within NATO, nuclear deterrence was non-rival and non-excludable giving rise to free riding. Weapons technology can also affect the mix of joint products by introducing new weapons into the deterrent—protective spectrum. For example, early warning systems, airborne weapon and control systems (AWACS) and satellite surveillance are purely protective weapons.

By 1967, NATO had shifted its defence strategy from nuclear deterrence to *flexible response* where aggression is met with a phased response of conventional and tactical nuclear forces before resorting to strategic nuclear forces. Flexible response meant that NATO's defence activities provided various types of joint products with different amounts of publicness.

The end of the Cold War led to further changes in NATO military strategy. It added a new focus on *crisis management and peacekeeping* resulting in new force structures. The terrorist attacks of 9/11 added a new threat dimension with additional concerns about weapons of mass destruction (WMD). A new strategic concept emerged in 2010 known as *Active Engagement, Modern Defence* which identified three core tasks for NATO, namely, collective defence, crisis management and co-operative security. Collective defence is based on Article 5 and deterrence is based on a mix of nuclear and conventional forces. Crisis management embraces the prevention and management of crises, the stabilisation of post-conflict situations and support for reconstruction. Co-operative security focuses on international security via co-operation and support for arms control, disarmament, non-proliferation and NATO enlargement. Interestingly, empirical tests of the impact on member's defence spending of the three major changes in NATO doctrine and policy were quite weak (Amara 2008).

New NATO force structures require choices between protection of national territory and boundaries and contributing forces for a NATO Rapid Reaction Force. For example, the procurement of light mobile weapons, the training of more mobile troops and the acquisition of air transport capabilities for rapid deployment means a substitution away from border-protecting forces in favour of rapid reaction forces. Force thinning arises where reinforcements in one place may lead to weaknesses elsewhere. Exploitation emerges in different forms such as smaller allies waiting for larger allies to acquire power-projecting capabilities (e.g. strategic airlifters): when a contingency arises, the larger allies have to transport the smaller allies troops and equipment to the conflict zone (Siqueira and Sandler 2001).

The joint product model can be applied to the proposed commitment by all NATO nations to increase defence spending to 2% of GDP by 2024. The target of a simple rise in defence spending allows each nation to allocate its defence resources according to its national preferences. On this basis, nations are likely to allocate the extra defence spending to forces which provide private benefits to each ally rather than public benefits to the alliance. There are further limitations of the NATO 2% target. It provides no indication of the optimal mix of spending. One critic has suggested an optimal mix of 40% on personnel and 25% on major equipment (Dowdy 2017).

There are distinctions between the joint product model and the deterrence model of alliances. First, a high ratio of excludable benefits to total benefits means that an alliance member must support its own defence regardless of its size. As this ratio approaches one, the exploitation hypothesis becomes less relevant. Second, alliance size restrictions depend on force thinning: allies with long exposed borders cause more thinning and must contribute a larger share of conventional forces (Sandler and Hartley 2001). Overall, most empirical studies supported the joint product model for the period of flexible response (Sandler and Hartley 1999, p. 48).

There are other models of alliances. One highlights the difference between a nation's internal defence burden and alliance membership burdens. Internal defence burdens are measured by defence shares of GDP which do not reflect the relative burdens and benefits of NATO membership. Alliance membership burdens involve any adverse changes in the threat resulting from alliance membership and alliance benefits comprise the reduction in the defence burden as defence spill-ins emerge from the other alliance members. Alliance membership in post-Cold War NATO provided public benefits when NATO members truly shared common interests in NATO's redefined roles and responsibilities; NATO's benefits are more private where members do not share these interests (Gates and Terasawa 2003).

Other alliance models have tested the relationship between defence spending or burdens and alternative measures of defence benefits. NATO's collective defence provides a range of benefits reflected in GDP and population which were used as proxies for the protection of human and physical capital (lives and industry saved). A further indicator for benefits was exposed borders which represented force thinning. However, doubts have been expressed about the validity of the exposed border and force thinning variable. For example, modern conflicts have made the concept of an exposed border irrelevant and NATO's primary concern is not the protection of the region's exposed borders. Omitting the exposed border variable from empirical studies raised doubts about its validity (Solomon 2004; Sandler 2005).

Different measures of burden-sharing and different tests produce different rankings. A study of NATO's long run defence burdens over the period 1949 to 2002 found that Greece and Turkey's aggregate defence burden index was the highest showing an increasing commitment to NATO over time, closely followed by Norway. It was recognised that Greece and Turkey were responding to defence concerns which were not shared by the remaining allies. An alternative country ranking index gave more conventional results showing the USA as first ranked followed by the UK, France and Germany (Amara 2007).

The 2% Target: Solution or Problem?

The agreement of NATO members to spend 2% of their national output on defence is presented as 'the solution' to the burden-sharing debates and US criticism of inadequate defence efforts by European states. But the 2% target is symbolic and needs to be subject to economic evaluation and critical appraisal.[4]

The 2% target has some attractive features. It is simple and easy to measure but fundamentally flawed. It creates the impression that NATO's problems are solved when they have not been addressed. The 2% figure focuses on defence *inputs* to the neglect of the more meaningful focus on defence *outputs*. The target is also open to misuse. For example, in 2015, the UK included £2.2 billion in its NATO military expenditure figures by adding military and civilian pensions spending, the UK's contribution to UN peace-keeping and a large proportion of income from other nations defence ministries. In other words, people adjust to targets and can play any games to achieve a target. Nor does the 2% target include non-monetary contributions to NATO defence and security. Examples include host nation provision of military bases and over-flying rights which need to be recognised in any assessment of defence burdens. Furthermore, the 2% target does not measure a nation's willingness to use military force; its trustworthiness in conflicts (e.g. in conflict will it turn up?); and the quality of its military capability. For example, is its equipment modern, serviceable and ready to use; and are its military personnel trained and ready for deployment? NATO's Readiness Initiative is far from impressive. It requires 30 battalions, 30 air squadrons and 30 combat ships to be ready for deployment within 30 days. This is a small force which takes about one month to assemble![5] It further raises the question of whether 2% is the correct figure or whether it should be 1% or 3%? Evaluating the defence implications of smaller and larger defence budgets would help to determine NATO's optimal defence expenditure.

The 2% target fails to show whether members are spending sufficient on repairs and maintenance. For example, in 2014, Germany recorded only 42 of 109 Typhoons, 38 of 89 Tornado aircraft and 4 of 22 Lynx

[4] The 2% target first appeared in a NATO Summit document at the NATO Wales Summit in 2014.

[5] Within these targets, the NATO Land Force 2008 target was for at least 50% of the Force to be deployable and 10% deployable on a sustained basis (but no definition was given of the length of sustained).

helicopters were ready for service due to a lack of spares. Nor can it be assumed that all nations, including the USA, are operating efficiently in their defence markets. NATO defence markets remain far from efficient: they are characterised by inefficient Armed Forces and inefficient defence industries with such inefficiency affecting the US and European defence markets. The 2% target diverts attention from the challenge of spending more efficiently rather than spending more. Chapter 5 addresses the efficiency challenge.

Is there a better alternative to the 2% target? It is not a perfect indicator and its limitations need to be recognised. However, if NATO members agree on a new burden-sharing indicator which might be a multi-variable measure, they need to specify the weights to be attached to each variable.

Conclusion

One commentator identified the future importance of the burden-sharing debate by suggesting that "NATO is ultimately strategic insurance against war in an unstable world in which strategy, technology, capability and affordability are combining for allies and adversaries alike. Europeans must realise that in the coming decade a hard-pressed US will only be able to 'guarantee' Europe's future defence if Europeans do far more for their own defence" (Lindley-French May, 2020). Economists focus on the affordability of NATO defence whilst recognising the relevance of strategy, technology and capability. But for NATO there remains the question of why and how did NATO survive the end of the Cold War? Chapter 4 uses public choice analysis to deal with this question.

References

Amara, J. (2007). Evaluating NATO Long Run Defense Burdens Using Unit Root Tests. *Defence and Peace Economics, 18*(2), 157–181.

Amara, J. (2008). NATO Defense Expenditures: Common Goals or Diverging Interests? A Structural Analysis. *Defence and Peace Economics, 19*(6), 449–469.

Beeres, R., & Bogers, M. (2012). Ranking the Performance of European Armed Forces. *Defence and Peace Economics, 23*(1), 1–16.

Dowdy, J. (2017, November). *More Tooth, Less Tail: Getting Beyond NATO's 2 Percent Rule.* London: McKinsey and Company.

Gates, W. R., & Terasawa, K. L. (2003). Reconsidering Publicness in Alliance Defence Expenditures: NATO Expansion and Burden Sharing. *Defence and Peace Economics, 14*(5), 369–383.

Hartley, K. (2011). *The Economics of Defence Policy*. London: Routledge.

Hartley, K., & Sandler, T. (1999). NATO Burden-Sharing: Past and Future. *Journal of Peace Research, 36*(6), 665–680.

Lindley-French, J. (2020, May 13). *Reflecting on NATO 2030*, Website.

NATO. (2019a, December). *Funding NATO*. Brussels: North Atlantic Treaty Organization.

NATO. (2019b). *Press Release, 25th June, 2019, Defence Expenditure of NATO countries (2012–2019)*. Brussels: NATO.

Olson, M. (1965). *The Logic of Collective Action*. Cambridge, MA: Harvard University Press.

Olson, M., & Zeckhauser, R. (1966). An Economic Theory of Alliances. *Review of Economics and Statistics, 48*(3), 266–279.

Sandler, T. (1992). *Collective Action: Theory and Applications*. Ann Arbor: University of Michigan Press.

Sandler, T. (2005). NATO Benefits, Burdens and Borders: Comment. *Defence and Peace Economics, 16*(4), 317–321.

Sandler, T., & Hartley, K. (1999). *The Political Economy of NATO*. Cambridge: Cambridge University Press.

Sandler, T., & Hartley, K. (2001). Economics of Alliances: The Lessons for Collective Action. *Journal of Economic Literature, XXXIX*(3), 869–896.

Siqueira, K., & Sandler, T. (2001). Models of Alliances: Internalizing Externalities and Financing. *Defence and Peace Economics, 12*(3), 249–270.

Solomon, B. (2004). NATO Burden Sharing Revisited. *Defence and Peace Economics, 15*(3), 251–258.

CHAPTER 4

NATO: An Economics, Politics and Public Choice Analysis

Abstract Public choice analysis is used to explain the survival of NATO. Key players in its survival are voters, political parties, bureaucracies and interest groups, especially producer groups.

Keywords Bureaucracies • Producer groups • Military-industrial-political complex

Introduction

Why and how did NATO survive the end of the Cold War and continues to this day? One possible explanation arises in the political market place where policy choices are made and implemented and which economists have traditionally regarded as a 'black box' so neglecting an important area of decision-making.

Government decisions are the result of actions by various agents and interest groups in the political market, each acting in their own self-interest and seeking to influence policy in their favour. The agents comprise voters, government, bureaucracies, producer and other interest groups. This chapter outlines the role of these agents and interest groups in determining the future of NATO, its survival and its defence policy. The approach shows how the public choice paradigm might be applied to the arguments used by different interest groups to justify the survival and continuation of NATO. Public choice analysis provides a framework for analysing the

K. Hartley, *NATO at 70*,
https://doi.org/10.1007/978-3-030-54395-2_4

military-industrial-political complex (MIPC) and its role in determining the future of NATO. Agents in the MIPC will influence defence policy including views about military threats, levels of defence spending, weapons acquisition programmes and the survival of NATO.

Some of these agents represent barriers to withdrawal from NATO and its abolition. Inevitably, questions arise as to who might gain and who might lose from a policy change and what arrangements, if any, will be made to compensate the potential losers? Clearly, those likely to lose will oppose any policy change, particularly if there are no arrangements for adequate compensation. Ultimately, society might regard a change as desirable only if the potential gainers are able to over-compensate the potential losers. Furthermore, the arrangements for transferring income between gainers and losers will be influenced by the agents in the political market.

The Political Market and Public Choice Analysis

The economist's approach to military spending stresses the 'public good' nature of defence and regards governments as maximising the welfare of society. With this approach, elected politicians and bureaucrats are assumed to pursue the 'public interest' and to implement the 'will of the people'. There are, however, problems in using the voting system to interpret society's preferences. It cannot be assumed that in public office, politicians and bureaucrats will behave in a 'saintly fashion', completely ignoring the opportunities for self-interest which they pursue in their private lives. Public choice analysis applies the ideas of self-interest and exchange to the political process. This approach shows that choices about defence and the survival of NATO are made in political markets (Buchanan 1986; Tisdell and Hartley 2008).

Political markets resemble other markets in that they contain buyers and sellers pursuing their self-interest by undertaking mutually beneficial exchange within the rules determined by the constitution. The agents within the political market comprise voters, political parties, bureaucracies, producer and other interest groups. These agents form the MIPC and each will have views on the future of NATO.

Voters

Within political markets, voters act like consumers and are assumed to seek the maximum benefit from the policies offered by rival politicians and political parties. However, voters have only limited information and knowledge about specialised military topics such as the threat, the survival and future of NATO, the levels of NATO collective defence spending, NATO standardisation and the merits of collaborative NATO defence equipment programmes.

Where the collection of specialist information is costly, there are opportunities for producers and other interest groups with specialist knowledge to influence voters and political parties. For example, national defence contractors form producer groups which can use their specialist knowledge to show that domestic purchasing is in the 'national interest', provides 'invaluable' independence and makes a socially desirable contribution to jobs, high technology and the balance of payments. The opportunities for producer groups to influence policy are reinforced by the limitations of the voting system as a means of accurately registering society's preferences.

Ideally, the individual tastes and preferences of large numbers of voters are recorded through the ballot box at elections. In some countries (e.g. UK), votes are cast for a general package of policies (an election manifesto) in which defence policy and NATO membership might be only one amongst a diverse set comprising economic, social, environmental, international and other policies between which voters cannot register the intensity of their preferences. Nor are voters provided with the necessary information to evaluate NATO and its defence policy. Secrecy and 'national security interests' mean` that voters are given little information about the contribution of different defence budgets to protection and security and the probability of survival in various conflict situations. Furthermore, voters cannot bind politicians to a clearly specified set of policies, which means that elected representatives have discretion in implementing their election promises. An elected party with, say, a commitment to withdraw from NATO can always delay the implementation of such commitments by claiming the principle of 'unripe time', the need for a thorough in-depth study and review of the issues, and the necessity of negotiating with their allies! All of which suggests that the limitations of the voting system as a means of accurately registering society's views on defence budgets and policies allows opportunities for governments, bureaucracies and other groups to interpret the 'national interest' and to influence national defence policy, including membership of NATO. Ultimately, though, governments cannot ignore the need to be re-elected.

Political Parties

Economic models of politics assume that political parties are vote-maximisers (Downs 1957). Like firms, parties offer policies in exchange for votes. Politicians are assumed to be self-interested, seeking the income, power and prestige which come from holding office, rather than seeking office to carry out preconceived policies. Politicians have the choice of joining one of the rival political parties or forming a new party. For example, opponents of NATO and supporters of reduced defence spending have to decide whether to influence party policy by attempting to change the policies of an established political party (c.f. a take-over) or by creating a new party. Both solutions involve costs. But, however attractive a specific defence policy might be to its supporters, it will never be implemented if the party fails to attract votes. Government supporters of NATO will stress the military advantages of collective defence and its contribution to lowering national defence costs. NATO can be presented by government as a force for good offering 'value for money' by providing collective and more defence at lower cost (Chap. 3). The winning party at an election captures the entire market and forms the government. Its policies are implemented by bureaucracies.

Bureaucracies

Economic models of bureaucracies start by assuming that bureaucrats are budget maximisers (Niskanen 1971). In the national defence market, the Defence Ministry or Department and the Armed Forces occupy a central role, with the Treasury concerned with the size of the defence budget and other Departments concerned with civil defence and the jobs, technology and balance of payments implications of defence spending. A government can be viewed as buying protection from the Defence Ministry which acts as a sole or monopoly supplier of information and defence, with protection supplied by the Armed Forces specialising in providing air, land and sea forces, and each seeking to protect its traditional monopoly property rights. To maximise its budget, the Defence Ministry can exaggerate the threat, underestimate costs and formulate programmes which are attractive to vote-maximising governments. Nevertheless, bureaucratic behaviour might be constrained by the activities of pressure groups and by the investigations of official scrutiny agencies (e.g. Parliamentary Defence and Public Accounts Committees; National Audit Office).

Bureaucrats enjoy the benefits of NATO membership. It is a military organisation which supports higher defence spending and can be used to support specific weapons programmes and provide opposition to the cancellation of projects. It also offers opportunities for international travel to attend meetings in attractive locations in Member States. The central management core of NATO forms a major pressure group which will oppose policies to abolish it: staff will lose their jobs if NATO is abolished. Similarly, national Armed Forces have a vested interest in the continuation of NATO: they benefit from being associated with a world-class international military alliance and with major allies such as the USA operating the latest high-tech military equipment (e.g. F-22 aircraft) and being involved in regular military exercises. Military personnel also benefit from overseas postings in Brussels and from attending meetings in foreign locations. The UK in particular gains unique benefits from NATO in the form of the 'special relationship' with the USA. This special relationship offers the UK military and economic benefits. Military benefits include the influence and prestige of being associated with the USA and being regarded as the number two nation in NATO. Economic benefits include access to the US defence market and partnership in major defence projects (e.g. F-35).

Producer Groups

In formulating and implementing policies, governments and bureaucracies are subject to the activities of pressure groups. Such groups of producers and consumers will pursue their self-interest by trying to influence policy in their favour through lobbying, advertising campaigns, sponsorship of politicians, consultancy reports, mass demonstrations and civil disobedience. The various interest groups will represent the potential gainers and losers from different defence and NATO policies.

Defence contractors form a major producer group which will be involved in formulating defence policy. They will seek monopoly profits or rents (rent seeking) from achieving a monopoly position through, say, contract awards or tariff protection in the defence market. Such groups will support the NATO aim of higher military spending and will lobby for government preferential purchasing from domestic defence contractors (e.g. a buy-British/French/German policy). Defence contractors will support collaborative defence equipment projects where groups of NATO Member States combine to build a new defence equipment project. Contractors will also seek favourable rules for regulating profits on defence work. Trade unions and professional associations with members in national defence industries will also support domestic arms producers so as to protect the jobs and favourable income prospects of their members. For example, faced with the cancellation of a major national defence project, it will be claimed that cancellation would involve writing-off large sums of taxpayer's money, losses of jobs, lost exports, as well as adverse effects on the future competitiveness of various sectors of domestic industry. It is not unknown for contractors to threaten the closure of plants, especially those in high unemployment areas and marginal constituencies. Such claims need to be assessed critically: what are their costs and the costs of alternative policies? There is a further aspect of rent-seeking behaviour by producers. Firms will lobby government for the award of major defence contracts so there are incentives to offer bribes to the officials who award the contracts. Bribes are not unknown in defence markets, especially in arms export markets (Mueller 1989, p. 231).

Other Pressure Groups

Other pressure groups in each national defence market represent specific consumer interests such as those in favour of disarmament (e.g. the Society of Friends); those opposed to nuclear weapons (e.g. CND; environmental groups); those opposed to specific conflicts; and those in favour of strong defences. Furthermore, a number of groups specialise in the independent evaluation of national defence policy, so providing voters and politicians with an alternative source of information outside the government bureaucracy. Examples include university research centres, the Brookings Institute, Rand, Chatham House and the International Institute for Strategic Studies. In addition to the agents in the domestic political market, the international community through such organisations as the European Union and the United Nations has an interest in the survival of NATO.

There are various formal and informal linkages between the different agents in the MIPC contributing to the survival of NATO. For example, civil servants and military personnel might be 'captured' by NATO and in return for supporting NATO they might be rewarded with jobs with defence contractors. But NATO survived and expanded with claims of new threats in a new World Order. These included threats below Article 5 level and out-of-area crisis management embracing peace-keeping, humanitarian and disaster relief. Questions then arise as to whether these are real and genuine threats or ones created by NATO to justify its survival? Problems arise in identifying evidence to test for the existence of the new threats. Possible answers might include evidence on the levels of Russian and Chinese military spending and their new weapons programmes (e.g. new missile developments). However, not all evidence on new threats is reliable. For example, evidence on the UK war with Iraq suggests that government can manipulate and falsify an enemy threat. For example, the Report on the Iraq Inquiry found that the threat posed by Saddam Hussein was deliberately exaggerated and Britain's intelligence agencies produced 'flawed' information about Saddam's weapons of mass destruction (Chilcott 2016).

Predictions of Public Choice Analysis

Public choice analysis suggests four predictions relevant to explaining the survival of NATO. First, in a two party electoral system, both parties agree on any issues strongly favoured by a majority of voters (i.e. the median voter). The result is consensus politics, with party policies being vague, similar to those of other parties and less directly linked to an ideology than in a multi-party system. Throughout much of the period since 1945, both UK major political parties offered similar policies on defence and on the continued membership and survival of NATO. However, there were periods (e.g. in the 1980s) when the major UK political parties offered radically different policies, particularly on nuclear weapons, on US military bases located in the UK and continued membership of NATO. However, the UK Labour Party of 1983 which was critical of NATO membership and its policies was not elected.

Second, although political parties attempt to differentiate their policies, movements towards the political extreme of the abolition of NATO is likely to be constrained by the potential losses of moderate voters. Political parties also tend to maintain consistent ideological positions over time, unless they suffer drastic defeats at which point they change their ideology to resemble that of the party which defeated them (Downs 1957).

Third, the policies of democratic governments tend to favour producers more than consumers. Examples include supporting the defence industrial base and regulations which benefit producers rather than consumers (e.g. by guaranteeing the profitability of defence contracts: Hartley 2018). Producer groups dominate since they can afford the costly investments in specialised information needed to influence government and they have the most to gain from influencing policy in their favour. Also, the voters who are best informed on any policy issue are those whose incomes are directly affected by the policy change (i.e. producer groups), whereas such citizens are not as well-informed on policies that affect them as consumers. As a result, producer groups, professional associations and trade unions, will support NATO and oppose policies for its abolition.

Fourth, the Armed Forces and bureaucracies aiming to maximise their budgets are likely to be too large and inefficient. They will exaggerate or over-estimate military threats. To protect and raise their budgets, Armed Forces and government departments which have a monopoly of specialist knowledge will use information to their advantage. Civil servants are experts: they have an infinite capacity for ingenuity and they can adjust and play any games. Fans of the television series *Yes, Prime Minister* will recognise the genre. Civil servants are specialists with technical information on the possibilities for varying output and for factor substitution. These possibilities, which could result in undesirable outcomes for vote-sensitive governments, might be too costly for any individual minister to police and monitor. In the circumstances, bureaucrats have an incentive to hoard valuable information and to erect a set of myths around their preferred policies. For example, as a buyer of defence services, the government often lacks alternative sources of specialist knowledge to monitor and evaluate military plans and military threats, as expressed in operational requirements for new weapons and new force structures as well as for the retention of NATO. The Armed Forces and bureaucracies have incentives to exaggerate the enemy's missile threat, the threats from such nations as China and Russia and the threats from international terrorists. Governments also lack independent advice on the reliability of the cost estimates of new equipment, and on whether a new weapon is worthwhile in terms of its marginal contribution to national defence. Bureaucracies also have every inducement to under-estimate the costs of their preferred policies and new weapons systems. They can support 'optimistic' cost estimates and neglect life-cycle costs (claiming that they are impossible to estimate). Once started, defence projects are difficult to stop. They attract interest groups of scientists, contractors, unions and military personnel, each with relative income gains from the continuation of the work. Indeed, it has been claimed that one of the benefits of international collaborative defence projects involving government (e.g. Tornado; Typhoon) is that they are much more difficult to cancel!

Some Applications

Public choice analysis offers some interesting insights and contributions to understanding the political process and policy formulation. Questions arise as to whether there is any evidence supporting the predictions of public choice analysis. There are some UK examples of empirical work based on cuts in military spending associated with Defence Reviews. A public choice approach identifies some of the agents most likely to oppose policies designed to reduce defence spending and to change its composition. It shows the type of arguments used by bureaucracies to protect budgets and how the armed forces and domestic defence contractors are likely to respond to cuts and programme cancellations. Such an evaluation also exposes to critical scrutiny some of the myths of defence and procurement policy. Ideally, though, public choice models need to be compared with alternative explanations of defence spending and policy formulation, aiming to discover which theory best explains the facts.

The UK Defence Reviews between 1957 and 2010 show at least three features which are consistent with public choice analysis. First, by aggregating modest annual savings in planned expenditure over a ten-year period, the Armed Forces and the Ministry of Defence were able to present an impressive picture of cuts, and a vote-sensitive government could show its supporters and the electorate that after a 'searching and thorough reappraisal of defence policy', it is taking 'firm, decisive action' involving 'tough choices' to reduce military spending. Often long-term contractual commitments to military manpower and equipment projects make it difficult and costly to achieve substantial cuts instantly. And, by offering sizeable future cuts, the Armed Forces and the Ministry of Defence can always hope for a change in the financial position or a transfer of the problem to their successors!

Second, the Armed Forces are major interest groups which will seek to protect their traditional property rights and their prestige and glamorous high technology weapons projects which often give satisfaction to their users rather than to society seeking protection and security. Faced with budget cuts, the Armed Forces are likely to respond by cutting reserve forces, civilians and economising on training, exercises, support functions and stocks, rather than sacrificing their major new equipment programmes.

Admirals like aircraft carriers, generals prefer tanks and air marshals enjoy air superiority fighters. As a result, preferences for inputs are likely to differ between the Armed Forces. The capital intensive air force will be willing to sacrifice, say, personnel and its transport aircraft fleet, including helicopters, rather than its latest combat aircraft. The labour-intensive army will aim to protect personnel as its most valuable asset, especially its elite combat forces, and it will sacrifice trucks for tanks and attack helicopters. Similarly, each service will be keen to show that it can undertake more cost-effectively roles currently undertaken by its rivals. For instance, the RAF will claim that its fleet of maritime patrol aircraft can replace some of the Navy's frigates in the anti-submarine role; and the Army will suggest that its attack helicopters can replace the RAF's close support aircraft.

Third, as a budget-conscious agency, the Ministry of Defence will oppose efforts to cut military spending. It will emphasise the 'dire consequences' of budget cuts, pointing to the continuing threat from nations such as China, Iran, Russia and North Korea, and the emerging threats from international terrorism and failed states. Stress will be placed on the employment and social consequences of cancelling weapons projects and closing military bases in remote rural areas lacking alternative job opportunities. References will also be made to the loss of national independence, prestige and high technology, resulting in the UK becoming a nation of 'metal bashers'. Other Government Departments concerned with employment, industry, technology and innovation as well as the Foreign Office are likely to support the arguments about jobs, technology and the international prestige of being a world military power (including the special relationship with the USA). Furthermore, some of these arguments might influence a vote-maximising government concerned about the electoral harm of defence cuts, particularly their impact on marginal constituencies. In turn, to protect itself and the Armed Forces against substantial budget cuts, the Ministry of Defence will promise future efficiency savings from better acquisition policies including competitive procurement, military outsourcing and greater rationalization within and between the armed forces This suggests that Defence Reviews might have a 'shock effect' leading to efficiency improvements. Some empirical tests of the shock effect hypothesis have concentrated on the manpower impact of Defence Reviews. It has been hypothesised that Defence Reviews will have a shock effect resulting in a once-and-for-all release of military and civilian manpower employed by the Armed Forces, the Ministry of Defence and the UK defence industries. With the possible exception of the Air Force, the evidence provided no support for a sudden shake-out of labour following a Defence Review (Hartley and Lynk 1983; Lynk and Hartley 1985).

Producer groups have a major role in public choice models and the MIPC. However, few efforts have been made to operationalise the concept of a producer group. Critics of military spending claim that defence contractors are a powerful and influential pressure group. On this basis, an analysis of the major UK defence firms and their market environment indicates that powerful producer groups have some of the following features:

1. *Firm size and market structure.* Firms are large in both absolute and relative size. Table 5.3 shows NATO's Top 25 arms firms in 2018 ranked by arms sales. US defence firms accounted for 15 of the Top 25 in 2018.
2. *Dependence on defence business.* Some defence firms and industries are highly dependent on Government defence contracts, so that their fortunes are closely linked with government decisions. Table 5.3 shows examples of defence dependency for the world's leading arms firms. In some cases, firms were 95% to 98% dependent on arms sales.
3. *Location.* Vote-sensitive governments seeking re-election are likely to be influenced by firms located in marginal constituencies or in high unemployment areas (e.g. shipbuilding).
4. *Types of contracts.* Firms awarded non-competitive contracts (e.g. cost-plus or incentive contracts) will have close and continuous links with the defence procurement agency. Here, it is possible that procurement policy, the type of contract and the arrangements for regulating defence profits were the result of successful lobbying by producer groups, with both contracts and profit rules favouring producers. However, the introduction of a competitive procurement policy changed the traditional 'cosy relationship' between the Defence Ministry and national defence industries (Hartley 2018).
5. *Lobbying activities.* This is another 'black box' which economists have neglected but it is a potentially important mechanism in the set of linkages in the political market. Defence contractors lobby as a group through specialist trade associations, such as those representing aerospace, electronics, engineering, naval equipment and defence manufacturers. Also, business appointments by staff leaving Defence Departments and the Armed Forces provide defence contractors with valuable contacts and expertise in their search for business.

Conclusion

Public choice analysis explains the survival of NATO in terms of the behaviour of interest groups in the military-industrial-political complex. Each group will pursue its objectives with governments seeking to maximise votes, bureaucracies in the form of the armed forces and defence ministries aiming to maximise budgets and producers seeking rents. The result of such behaviour is the survival of NATO.

The analysis identifies the agents in the MIPC which will seek to influence defence policy and determine the future of NATO. It shows how groups which will lose from the abolition of NATO are likely to behave and the arguments which will be used to oppose such a policy. The approach seems to offer a realistic description of the world. But descriptive reality and intuitive appeal are not sufficient for the acceptance of a theory. Does the approach offer any clear, testable predictions and does the evidence support these predictions? If there are alternative explanations of NATO's survival, it is necessary to determine whether the public choice approach is superior and out-performs existing models which ignore the political market.

For example, Marxist economists claim that military spending is necessary for the maintenance of capitalism as a viable system, both nationally and internationally. In contrast, standard economic theory analyses defence spending as an optimisation problem in which defence output as a public good is maximised subject to the available resource constraints. Alternatively, public choice analysis explains defence spending in terms of the maximising behaviour of governments, bureaucracies and interest groups in the MIPC. Analysts have the task of identifying alternative predictions from these different explanations or adopting an eclectic approach using elements from each model.

Inefficiency in NATO has also been criticised. Public choice analysis provides an explanation for such inefficiency.

References

Buchanan, J. (1986). *Liberty, Market and the State*. London: Harvester.

Chilcott, S. J. (2016). *The Report of the Iraq Inquiry*. London: TSO.

Downs, A. (1957). *An Economic Theory of Democracy*. New York: Harper and Row.

Hartley, K. (2018). The Profitability of Non-Competitive Defence Contracts: The UK Experience. *Defence and Peace Economics, 29*(6), 577–594.

Hartley, K., & Lynk, E. (1983, February). Labour Demand and Allocation in the UK Engineering Industry: Disaggregation, Structural Change and Defence Reviews. *Scottish Journal of Political Economy, 30*(1), 42–53.
Lynk, E., & Hartley, K. (1985). Input Demands and Elasticities in UK Defence Industries. *International Journal of Industrial Organization, 3*, 71–83.
Mueller, D. C. (1989). *Public Choice II*. Cambridge: Cambridge University Press.
Niskanen, W. (1971). *Bureaucracy and Representative Government*. Chicago: Aldine-Atherton.
Tisdell, C., & Hartley, K. (2008). *Microeconomic Policy*. Cheltenham: Elgar.

CHAPTER 5

NATO and Europe: Improving Efficiency

Abstract The chapter provides details on European defence policy and the scope for improving efficiency and the impact on NATO. The features of defence industries are presented and the challenge of developing an efficient defence industrial policy in an alliance. Collaboration and its inefficiencies are reviewed.

Keywords Defence industries • Collaboration • Action Plan

Introduction

Europe's position in NATO raises efficiency and burden-sharing issues. This chapter focuses on efficiency issues. Efficiency is defined, defence markets are described and defence industries are reviewed. European defence policy is outlined and analysed, including its potential impact on the future of NATO. If European defence and defence industrial policy are successful, they might create an alternative to NATO with the possibility of the EU leaving NATO.

Understanding the efficiency issue starts from the fact that NATO members are independent nation states and not a single unitary (e.g. UK) or Federal state (e.g. the USA). As a result, there is no single political entity for the whole of NATO and it is an organisation which has to pursue its objectives subject to the constraints of nation states. Expressed

K. Hartley, *NATO at 70*,
https://doi.org/10.1007/978-3-030-54395-2_5

more formally, it seeks to maximise defence output subject to national constraints. These constraints take the form of national preferences (e.g. for independence), national defence budgets, national armed forces and national defence industries. Public choice analysis shows how political factors form policy constraints. Interest groups of defence ministries, armed forces and defence firms seeking budgets, incomes and rents have incentives to identify the military and economic benefits of buying weapons from domestic suppliers (e.g. jobs, technology, export benefits) which is the source of inefficiency in NATO defence markets.

Efficiency is central to economics and focuses on least-cost solutions. In principle, such solutions are achieved in defence markets which bring together buyers and sellers of defence equipment. But defence markets depart drastically from the economists' competitive model which achieves economically efficient outcomes (a Pareto optimum where it is impossible to make one person better off without making someone else worse off). Defence markets have some distinctive features, namely, governments are major or monopsony buyers[1] and often there is a national monopoly supplier. Efficiency in defence markets can be improved in three ways. First, where two or more nations agree to form a *free trade area or a customs union* including defence equipment (an international trade agreement). The economic benefits of such trading arrangements apply to purchases of all defence equipment reflected in lower prices from competition and scale effects. Governments will remain major or monopsony buyers but monopoly or oligopoly suppliers can be subject to state regulation to 'improve' their performance (e.g. regulation of prices and profits). Second, two or more governments can agree to combine their national orders to buy one or all types of defence equipment (e.g. aircraft; tanks). The economic benefits of *cooperative purchasing* include increased bargaining power relative to the contractor and lower prices from scale effects. Third, two or more nations might agree to collaborate for the development and production of one type of defence equipment (e.g. aircraft; helicopters; missiles). This is supply-side cooperation where there are economic benefits from sharing costly development and economies of scale and learning from combining production orders. Overall, improved efficiency in defence markets can result from international trade based on specialisation by comparative

[1] Monopsony is a single buyer. An example is the demand for strategic nuclear submarines which are bought by national governments (e.g. France; UK; USA).

advantage (known as gains from trade)[2] and/or from lower unit costs reflecting scale and learning economies. Here, problems arise where efficiency is defined from a cost or supply-side perspective. This approach ignores demand-side perspectives and a buyers willingness to pay for a commodity: efficiency has a role for buyers and the valuation they place on their specific demands or preferences.[3]

Features of Defence Industries

Defence industries have some distinctive features which explain their conduct and performance. These include:

1. *Research and development (R&D) is costly* forming total fixed costs. Such total fixed costs have to be spread over a large output to reduce average unit R&D costs within total unit acquisition costs (i.e. development and production costs together form acquisition costs).
2. *The importance of quantity.* Defence industries are often decreasing cost industries meaning that unit costs decline with greater quantities. More specifically, production leads to economies of scale and learning so lowering average production costs. For example, learning economies in the aerospace industry result in a reduction of 5–10% in unit production costs for every doubling of cumulative output.
3. *Development costs are related to unit production costs for each type of equipment.* For combat aircraft, the ratio of total development costs to unit production cost might be 100–200:1; for helicopters, the ratio might be 120:1; for large fixed wing aircraft such as transports, tankers or electronic platform aircraft, the ratio might be 40:1; for air defence missiles, the ratio might be 500:1; and for armoured fighting vehicles, it might be a ratio of 250:1 (Pugh 2007).
4. *Cost trends.* Famously, Norman Augustine identified a trend of rising unit costs for advanced technology defence equipment. He forecast that unit cost trends were closely correlated with time rather than other

[2] Free trade areas and customs unions can lead to gains from trade but some trade effects divert trade rather than create gains. Examples occur where tariffs lead to trade being diverted to higher cost sources of supply.

[3] Consider the optimal use of private household toilets. A cost side perspective requires maximum use to minimise unit costs; but an allocatively efficient solution requires the minimum cost use preferred and chosen by consumers (including availability when required). In other words, allocative efficiency includes both demand and cost considerations.

explanatory factors such as speed, weight or manoeuvrability. More specifically, he forecast real unit costs rising by a factor of four every ten years for high-performance fighter and bomber aircraft as well as helicopters. The upward trend also applied to other high technology equipment such as ships and tanks but at a lower magnitude, namely, a growth factor of two every ten years. The result was the forecast of a single ship navy, a single tank army and Starship Enterprise or Battlestar Galactica for the air force (Augustine 1987; Hartley 2020; Kirkpatrick 1995).

5. *Defence equipment is costly.* For example, unit production costs for an aircraft carrier might be £8 billion, a nuclear-powered submarine might cost almost £3 billion per unit, a tank about £6 million, a strategic bomber £3.7 billion and an advanced combat aircraft over £100 million per copy (2019 prices: Hartley 2020). Examples are shown in Table 5.1. In addition to production costs, there are development costs. Both cost levels and trends provide incentives for weapons standardisation and collaboration.

Defence Industrial Policy in a Military Alliance

There is a considerable literature on the economics of military alliances focusing on their public goods benefits from collective defence, burden-sharing and free riding issues. Much less attention has been given to the opportunities for formulating an efficient defence industrial policy in an alliance. A starting point is the view that NATO is an inefficient military organisation with inefficiency embracing both its armed forces and defence industries. These are characterised by costly duplication in both spheres. In contrast, the former Warsaw Pact was often viewed as an efficient arms procurement organisation. Its efficiency resulted from central control of its armed forces which specialised in specific military roles and capabilities and its acquisition of a few standard types of defence equipment so allowing volume production. As a result, it avoided duplication of costly equipment developed and produced in small quantities. Overall military decision-making and allocation choices were the responsibility of the former Soviet Union which imposed its weapons choices on all Member States of the former Warsaw Pact.

Using the Warsaw Pact as a comparator, NATO appeared to be an inefficient military alliance. Each Member State deployed an independent

Table 5.1 Defence equipment costs: levels and growth

Equipment type	*Absolute cost (£s 2019 prices)*	*Annual rate of cost increase (%)*
Sea systems		
Aircraft Carrier	8.0B	3
Air Defence ship	934 mn	2
Submarine: SSBN (launch of nuclear missiles)	2.8B	NS
SSN (hunter-killer)	1.9B	1
Land		
Main Battle Tank	5.8 mn	1
Armoured Personnel Carrier	876 K	2
Air		
Fighter/Strike Aircraft	102 mn	4
Bomber Aircraft (strategic)	3.7B	10
Primary Trainer Aircraft	8.8 mn	7
Advanced Trainer Aircraft	24.8 mn	4
Military Transport/Tanker Aircraft	292 mn	4
Reconnaissance UAV	36.5 K	6
Attack Helicopter	35 mn	5
Anti-Submarine Helicopter	29 mn	6
Transport Helicopter	23.4 mn	4
Small arms		
Rifle	2.2 K	2
Machine Gun	5.1 K	NS
Missiles		
Cruise Missile	6.6 mn	8
Ballistic Missile	58 mn	5

Source: Pugh (2007)

Notes: (i) NS is not statistically significant; (ii) absolute costs in constant 2019 prices in pounds sterling: K is thousands, mn is millions and B is billions. Constant prices are based on the UK Retail Price Index; (iii) unit cost figures include development costs for warships (i.e. total acquisition costs comprising development and production). For all other equipment, unit costs are for unit production costs (i.e. excluding development cost); (iv) cost increases are in specific costs: £s per ton for ships; £s per tonne for tanks and personnel carriers; and £s per kilogram for aircraft and missiles. Cost figures are median values; (v) cost data are based on projects worldwide for which there is published data but most projects are from the USA and Europe.

army, navy and air force with duplication between them (e.g. national Defence Ministries; duplication of military bases; training; support facilities). National defence industries each developed and produced costly equipment for their national needs with costly duplication and short production runs. Economic principles for an efficient military force and defence markets suggest an optimal military alliance based on specialisation by comparative advantage for both armed forces and defence industries. On this basis, the USA might specialise in providing costly assets and military forces such as a complete range of strategic and tactical nuclear forces, strategic bombers, satellite surveillance, strategic tanker aircraft and ballistic missile defence. France and the UK might specialise in providing air defence, anti-submarine capabilities and a limited range of strategic nuclear forces; the UK might focus on special forces, aerial tankers and short take-off and vertical landing aircraft; Germany could provide armoured forces; Greece, Italy, Spain and Turkey might supply land forces; with the Netherlands and Norway providing naval escort forces.

The principle of specialisation by comparative advantage can also be applied to defence industries. On this basis, the US defence industry might specialise in high technology defence equipment such as aircraft, helicopters, missiles and space systems; France might specialise in combat aircraft; the UK might focus on aero-engine technology, armoured fighting vehicles and warships; Germany would specialise in tanks and submarines; and Italy in helicopters.

Two aspects of these proposals have to be addressed. First, the principle of specialisation requires trust between Member States. In the absence of a political union, Member States in a military alliance will prefer to retain their national independence reflected in an independent military force and national defence industry. Put simply, with specialisation based on comparative advantage, nations need to be certain that other Member States with their specialist military capability will turn-up in a conflict. Second, efficiency embraces both economic and technical efficiency. Economic efficiency does not necessarily mean weapons standardisation. Instead, it means that different national preferences in a military alliance are satisfied which suggests that duplication can be an efficient solution. Technical efficiency requires that production is undertaken on the lowest possible cost curve (X-efficient cost levels). In the Warsaw Pact model, it was assumed that production costs were minimised; but, in the absence of competition and the profit motive, Warsaw Pact production might have been X-inefficient (i.e. not least-cost). In contrast, privately owned and competitive NATO defence industries might operate at lower unit production costs even with smaller volumes compared with the Warsaw Pact.

Figures 5.1(a) and (b) show an analytical framework for illustrating the relative cost positions of NATO and Warsaw Pact nations. Figure 5.1 (a) presents a single unit cost curve showing the cost advantages of large-scale

Fig. 5.1 (a) Single cost curve; and (b) different cost curves

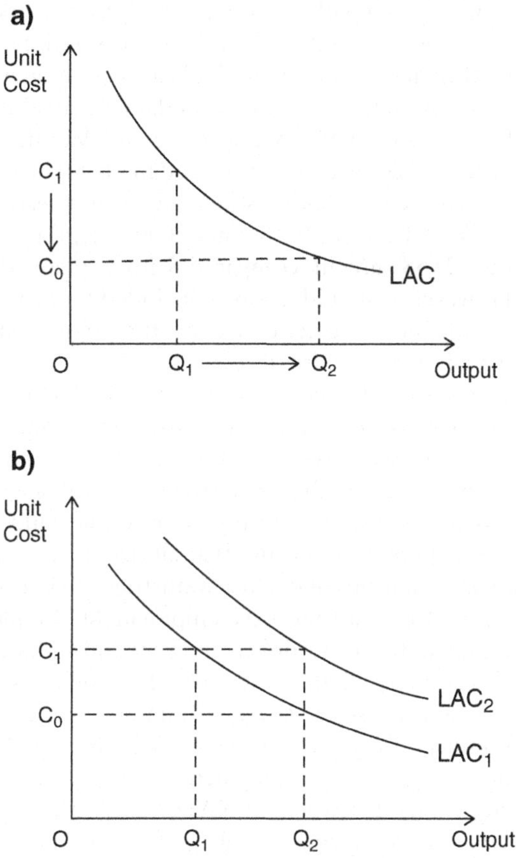

output. Figure 5.1 (b) shows different cost curves for NATO and the Warsaw Pact nations with cost curve LAC_2 being the unit cost curve for the Warsaw Pact nations and LAC_1 being the unit cost curve for NATO nations. In this case, Warsaw Pact output is Q_2 produced at a unit cost of C_1; but NATO with a smaller output of Q_1 producing on a lower unit cost curve can achieve the same unit costs as the Warsaw Pact (C_1). If through standardisation, NATO could achieve a larger output of Q_2, unit costs would fall to C_0. These cost curves show the benefits of large-scale production from economies of scale and learning and the gains from trade leading to lower unit costs.

Compared with the USA, EU defence markets appear to be inefficient in the provision of both armed forces and defence equipment. European inefficiency is reflected in duplication of military forces and defence industrial capabilities, all based on relatively small national markets.[4] The USA has a single army, navy, air force and Marine Corps providing large-scale orders creating a large domestic market which allows US defence firms to achieve economies of scale, scope and learning. For example, for the Lockheed Martin F-35 combat aircraft, the three US services planned to buy 2663 aircraft compared with a planned UK buy of 138 aircraft. However, it should not be concluded that larger US scales of output necessarily mean greater efficiency: the US Armed Forces and defence industry might also be inefficient.

To assess the relative size of NATO defence industries, data are needed on such size indicators as industry sales and employment. There are the inevitable data problems since there is a general absence of government-supplied data on the size of their national defence industries. Industry size can be measured in terms of arms sales and employment, but it is not always possible to ensure that all size data are based on standard and uniform definitions of defence industries, their arms sales and identical definitions of defence industry employment. Employment data vary between numbers based on direct, indirect and induced jobs and it is not always clear which definitions are used. Data on the size of NATO defence industries and those in Russia, China and Sweden all based on employment numbers are shown in Table 5.2. The USA clearly dominates NATO defence industry employment as well as comparable numbers for Russia and China. Elsewhere in NATO, there are major defence industries in the UK, France, Germany, Italy and Spain (Hartley and Belin 2020).

The European Defence Industrial Problem

A visitor from Mars would be astonished at the massive inefficiencies in European defence markets and industries. They are characterised by small national markets, duplication of costly R&D and national production orders which are 'too small' to achieve economies of scale and learning.

[4] Using Fig. 5.1(b), the US scale of output on LAC_1 could be Q_2 and unit costs of C_0 compared with a smaller European national output of Q_1 on LAC_2 and unit costs of C_1. Or, a worst case scenario might place the European nation on a higher cost curve above LAC_2 with unit costs higher than C_1.

Table 5.2 NATO defence industries

Country	*Employment numbers*
USA	2.3–4.1 million
UK	260,000
France	200,000
Germany	90,000–120,000
Italy	50,000
Turkey	44,740
Spain	40,000
Canada	27,000–59,800
Poland	20,000
Norway	6700
Greece	5210
Others:	
Russia	1.3 million–2 million
China	1.7 million
Sweden	30,000

Source: Hartley and Belin (2020)

Note: (i) Data are for 2016/2017; (ii) range of numbers shows direct numbers (lower figures) and direct plus indirect employment (higher numbers). Figures are rounded; (iii) data not available for all NATO Member States

The resulting European defence industrial problem is that each European nation is unable to compete with its US rivals. The desire for European solutions has led to various historical institutional initiatives of varying degrees of success and failure.

Developing a European Defence Policy and Armaments Agency

Following earlier initiatives, the European Union's Common Security and Defence Policy (CSDP) was agreed in 1999 involving military and civilian missions for peace, conflict prevention and international security. The EU and NATO have agreed a strategic partnership: 22 EU Member States are also NATO allies.

Various efforts have also been made at European arms cooperation and the creation of a European armaments agency. This was reflected in a standard rhetoric focusing on a desire to strengthen the European Defence Technological and Industrial Base (EDTIB), to cooperate in defence R&D, to open-up national defence markets and to promote a more efficient use of resources through harmonising equipment requirements. The eventual aim was to promote arms co-operation by creating a single European Armaments Agency.

An initiative came in 1996 with the creation of OCCAR known as the Organisation Conjointe de Cooperation pour l'Armement or the Organisation for Joint Armament Co-operation. This agency specialises in managing collaborative defence equipment projects. Originally, OCCAR involved four nations, namely, France, Germany, Italy and the UK (effective legally in January 2001) but later, Belgium and Spain joined. Programmes managed by OCCAR include the A400M airlifter, the Boxer armoured fighting vehicle, COBRA (weapon locating system), FREM (France-Italy Frigate programme) and the Tiger helicopter (see Table 5.5).

Single Market and EDTIB

Current European defence industrial policy is based on policy initiatives for the European Defence Agency (EDA), the European Defence Technology and Industrial Base (EDTIB) and the Single Market. EDA was created in 2004. It is an inter-governmental agency of the European Council comprising most Member States (except for Denmark). It partly reflected pressure from European aerospace and defence firms for a strong armaments agency able to overcome the deficiencies of previous initiatives in the field (e.g. OCCAR). Originally, EDA was tasked with developing defence capabilities for crisis management, promoting European arms cooperation, strengthening the EDTIB and creating a competitive European defence equipment market. Also, it was viewed eventually as a possible central European purchasing agency.

EDA has special responsibility for developing a European DTIB viewed as something more than the sum of its separate national parts. It regards national equipment requirements, duplicate and costly national R&D programmes and small-scale national procurement as economically unsustainable. Instead, EDA is tasked with creating an EDTIB which is capability-driven, competent and competitive within and outside Europe (the three Cs). It expects centres of excellence to emerge from a market-driven process, moderated by policy considerations including the requirement to achieve an appropriate regional distribution; but originally, it did not envisage a future EDTIB as a 'Fortress Europe' (EDA 2007, pp. 1–2).

The European Commission has a central role in creating a Single Market for the procurement of defence equipment (European Defence Equipment Market: EDEM). This is being achieved by a series of Defence

Procurement Directives aimed at promoting greater competition by opening national defence markets to cross border competition. The creation of the EDEM requires an appropriate legal framework specifying the rules for contract awards: for example, contracts awarded on the basis of the most economically advantageous offer. In the European Commission's view, the relationship between the EDEM and EDTIB involves the gradual establishment of the EDEM as essential for strengthening the EDTIB: the view is that closed and fragmented national defence markets create extra costs and inefficiencies which have negative impacts on the competitiveness of the EDTIB (EC 2009).

There are, though, major constraints on the creation of the EDEM. These take the form of specific exemptions from the Single Market rules which allow for the protection of a nation's essential security interests when purchasing arms, ammunition and war materials, including intelligence services. These exemptions were reflected initially in Article 296 which was replaced by Article 346 in 2009.

The European Commission issues Defence Procurement Directives aiming to create a more open, competitive and efficient European defence equipment market. Such a Market is expected to "help suppliers to achieve economies of scale, optimise production capacity and lower unit production costs, thus making European products more competitive on the global market. This should, in turn, strengthen the competitiveness of European defence industry, by fostering consolidation across national boundaries, helping to reduce duplication, and enhancing industrial specialisation" (EC 2016, p. 14).

Problems arose because Member States used exemptions, especially Articles 296 and 346, to ensure that the procurement of military equipment was not subject to EU public procurement rules aimed at 'opening-up' national defence markets. In reality, derogations which should have been the exceptions became the rule. In 2016, the Commission reviewed whether Articles 296 and 346 continued to form major barriers to creating a Single Market in defence equipment: a very significant share of defence procurement expenditure was being made outside the Defence Procurement Directive. It concluded that the objectives of the Directive had only partly been achieved and that its application remained uneven across Member States. Nor was there any evidence that overall, the Directive had fundamentally changed the development of the EDTIB and enabled SMEs to be more successful in winning defence contracts. Overall, the Commission found that a significant share of defence procurement expenditure was still undertaken outside of the Directive. Often, Member States used offsets/industrial return requirements under Article 346 to justify their reluctance to award defence contracts on the basis of competition.

The typical European Commission response to identifying problems in creating a Single Market is to formulate more legal procurement rules aimed at achieving compliance and 'good' behaviour. In this context, actions are required on concerns about security of supply, offsets and on sub-contracting. Further concerns arise from the opportunities for discriminatory technical specifications which favour national suppliers. Policy implementation is achieved by the threat of sanctions through references to the European Court of Justice. However, a new policy initiative was announced in late 2016, namely, the Action Plan for European Defence.

The Action Plan

The European Defence Action Plan of November 30th, 2016 outlined specific proposals to support a strong and innovative European defence industry and defence capabilities agreed by EU states. The Plan has three components. First, a *European Defence Fund* for collaborative research projects and the joint development of defence equipment and technologies. Second, supporting investments in *defence supply chains*, especially through finance for SMEs and encouraging the development of regional clusters of excellence. Third, ensuring that Europe has an open and competitive *Single Market* for defence. Overall, the Action Plan was viewed originally as a 'game changer' for more European defence co-operation (EC 2016). A related development was the creation in 2017 of PESCO or Permanent Structured Cooperation which allows Member States to pursue structural military and defence integration through shared initiatives and the pooling of resources. It is designed to fill capability gaps in areas such as cyber and joint training.

The European Defence Fund was a major initiative involving both research and capability windows. The research window will fund collaborative research on innovative defence technologies such as electronics, metamaterials, encrypted software or robotics. For 2017, the Commission proposed an initial research budget of Euros 25 million rising to a planned total of Euros 500 million per year after 2020. The capability window will provide funds for Member States to acquire and jointly own specific and costly assets, with a possible budget of Euros 5 billion per year. This window aims to provide joint funding of development and procurement of strategic capabilities (i.e. prototypes, development and procurement of products and technologies resulting from the research window).

The European Defence Action Plan aims to address the lack of interoperability, technology gaps and insufficient scale and learning economies in production. Some 80% of European defence procurement and 90% of defence research and technology is undertaken on a national basis. The resulting fragmentation of European defence equipment markets has led to Europe being less competitive than the US defence industry. For example, Europe has 180 different types of equipment compared with 30 for the USA. This total includes 29 types of frigates versus 4 in the USA; 17 types of battle tanks versus one in the USA; 20 types of fighter aircraft in Europe compared with 6 in the USA; 20 types of European armoured fighting vehicles compared with 2 in the US; and 13 types of European air-to-air missiles compared with 3 in the USA (EC 2016)

Since 1986, there has been a reduction in the number of major European arms firms. The number of main battle tank producers declined from 13 in 1986 to 6 in 2016; for combat aircraft, numbers declined from 16 firms in 1986 to 6 firms in 2016; and for warships the corresponding numbers were from 16 firms in 1986 to 8 firms in 2016. The lack of European arms co-operation was reflected in the costs of non-Europe in defence which was estimated to cost annually between Euros 25 billion and Euros 100 billion. This is because of inefficiencies, lack of competition and lack of economies of scale in production. Some 80% of European defence procurement is undertaken on a national basis leading to costly duplication of military capabilities (EC 2016).

The Action Plan appears to be a major improvement on previous policy initiatives. The EU has earmarked budgets for defence research and capabilities. But, appearances are deceptive. The collaborative research budget is small, even after 2020 and achieving the capability budget will be even more demanding. The costs of funding the 2020 corona virus pandemic and the associated economic recovery will affect adversely the size of future European defence budgets. Delays in implementation will follow and over time, the Action Plan will be quietly forgotten as yet another failed EU defence initiative. There is also the problem of determining spending priorities within the Action Plan. Inevitably, European defence choices will be the result of preferences reflected by its Member States where there are incentives to free ride and shift costs to the larger nations. The resulting defence priorities will reflect compromises and bargaining skills and not necessarily an assessment of the 'true' threats facing Europe: outcomes will reflect the bargaining environment of a political club. Ultimately, however, only nation states have the final responsibility for their national defence: they are responsible for assessing threats and providing security and protection for their citizens. European defence solutions require a single European state able to provide a single agreed view of threats to Europe and their solutions. Without a single European state, the inefficiency of national state solutions will continue to be reflected in the costly duplication of military capabilities and defence industries. Problems arise since the European Commission and its agencies are applying a model of a non-existent single European state to a large set of independent national European states. The challenge for the EU is to create the market and industry structures of a single market based on a group of Member States which act as autonomous and independent nations. The so-called problems of fragmentation and duplication of costly R&D arise from applying a non-existent and hypothetical model of a single European nation to the reality of independent nation states.

European Defence Industries

The starting point of the European Action Plan in assessing European defence industries is the lack of co-operation, with most defence research and defence procurement operated on a national basis. The European Action Plan aims to change this outcome by promoting and funding collaborative defence research and technology. Further efforts to promote European defence co-operation through the Action Plan are based on developing the capability window. Descriptive statistics for the major European defence firms and European defence expenditures are shown in Tables 5.3 and 5.4; data for European defence *industries* are shown in Table 5.2.

Data on the top 25 arms firms in NATO are shown in Table 5.3. American arms firms accounted for five of the top six in 2018 with only one European firm in the top six (BAE Systems). Similarly, there were 15 US firms in the top 25 in NATO compared with 10 European firms in the top 25. The average size of the US arms firms in the top 25 was almost twice the average size of the top European firms in the top 25. These size differences suggest substantial excess capacity in the European arms industry. For example, with US productivity levels for their top 15 applied to the total output from the top 10 European firms, then this output could

Table 5.3 NATO top 25 arms firms, 2018

Company	*Nation*	*Arms sales (US$ millions)*	*Arms sales as share of total sales (%)*
Lockheed Martin	USA	47,260	88
Boeing	USA	29,150	29
Northrop Grumman	USA	26,190	87
Raytheon	USA	23,440	87
General Dynamics	USA	22,000	61
BAE Systems	UK	21,210	95
Airbus Group	Trans-European	11,650	15
Leonardo	Italy	9820	68
Thales	France	9470	50
United Technologies Corporation	USA	9310	14
L3 Technologies	USA	8250	81
Huntington Ingalls Industries	USA	7200	88
Honeywell International	USA	5430	13
Leidos	USA	5000	49
Harris Corporation	USA	4970	73
Booz Allan Hamilton	USA	4680	70
Rolls-Royce	UK	4680	22
Naval Group	France	4220	99
Rheinmetall	Germany	3800	52
MBDA	Trans-European	3780	100
General Electric	USA	3650	3
Textron	USA	3500	25
CACI International	USA	3490	70
Safran	France	3240	13
Babcock	UK	3180	46
Average US ($n = 15$)	USA	13,568	70
Average European ($n = 10$)	European	7505	51

Source: SIPRI (2020)

Notes: (i) Based on SIPRI Top 100 arms producers in 2018; (ii) arms shares for average US and European firms are based on medians; (iii) subsidiaries are excluded; (iv) Saab is excluded since Sweden is not a NATO member. Saab sales in 2018 were $3240 mn, placing it in the same rank position as Safran

be produced by about 5 US-equivalent firms rather than the current ten European firms. Also, in 2018, American firms were more dependent on arms sales than their European equivalents: median arms sales shares of 70% in the USA and 51% in Europe.

Table 5.4 European defence spending, 2014 Euros, millions

Country	*Defence R&T*	*Defence R&D*	*Equipment procurement expenditure*	*European collaborative defence R&T spending*	*Collaborative equipment procurement as share of total equipment procurement (%)*
France	764	3563	6134	123	33
Germany	483	846	3781	NA	NA
Italy	0	103	1956	5	40
Poland	10	217	1811	2	2
Spain	42	75	1258	21	65
Sweden	61	106	1178	9	9
UK	493	3753	6553	1	28
All EU	*1953*	*8791*	*25897*	*170*	*22*

Source: EDA (2016)

Notes: (i) R&T is research and technology; R&D is research and development; equipment procurement is defence equipment procurement expenditure; (ii) European totals are for all Member States of the EDA. NA is not available. All data in Euros millions

BAE Systems was the largest European arms firm but it was considerably smaller than Lockheed Martin as the world's largest arms firm in 2018. The remaining major European arms firms were even smaller relative to Lockheed Martin. The top European firms had varying degrees of dependency on arms sales, ranging from as little as 13% (Safran) to almost 100% dependency (Naval Group) with a median of some 50% arms dependency. In comparison, Lockheed Martin had a defence dependency of some 88%.

European defence spending is concentrated in a small number of nations, namely, France, Germany, Italy, Poland and the UK. These five nations accounted for some 80% of European procurement spending. The degree of concentration was greater for EU defence R&D spending, with France and the UK accounting for about 80% of such expenditure. However, the figures are misleading since the EU *totals* are based on all Member States when the reality is that the total comprises a set of independent nation states and not a single EU state. In contrast, the USA forms a single Federal state where its defence R&D and procurement spending are designed to provide defence capabilities for the armed forces of the single nation state and not for each of the constituent states of the

US Federation. Also, the data show the dominance of the UK in the EU totals and the possible impact of Brexit on EU defence. The UK is a major defence market within the EU, with BAE forming Europe's largest arms company. The UK has also been a major participant in European collaborative equipment programmes.

Is Collaboration the Answer?

Collaboration is a major feature of the European Defence Action Plan embracing both collaborative defence research and procurement. The simple economics of collaboration appear attractive. Compared with a single nation solution, the theory of ideal or perfect collaboration offers the prospect of cost savings from sharing fixed R&D costs and lower unit production costs from combining production orders. For example, two equal nations would share R&D costs and combine their production orders to double output leading to greater scale and learning economies. On this basis, a collaborative project's R&D costs of, say, Euros 10 billion would be shared equally between two nations with each contributing Euros 5 billion (a 50% saving or Euros 5 billion for each nation). In addition, if each nation required, say, 100 units, then the total order would double from 100 units to 200 units, leading to possible reductions of 5–10% in unit production costs. Further national cost savings would be available if the number of partner nations increased from, say, two to four or six or more.

Reality departs from the ideal model. Compared with a national project, actual collaboration leads to inefficiencies resulting from the work-sharing arrangements. Each partner nation will demand its 'fair' share of the high technology work on the project. For example, on collaborative aerospace projects, each nation will demand an involvement in high technology work on the airframe, engine and avionics. Partner nations will each require a flight test centre. The resulting work-sharing based on equity criteria will not be economically efficient. Such inefficiencies are accentuated where a partner nation lacks the relevant technology and uses collaboration to fund the acquisition of new knowledge (which might already exist amongst other partner nations). The costs of acquiring the technology will be shifted to the other partner nations and its taxpayers. Further collaboration inefficiencies arise in production work. Each partner nation will demand a 'fair' share of production work, including a national final assembly line, leading to duplicate final assembly lines. And, some production work might be awarded to a partner nation to fulfil its work-sharing requirements across the collaborative project, even where the partner might lack competitiveness in the relevant field.

Collaboration inefficiencies also arise from the industrial management arrangements (the supply side). Partner nation governments will specify which of their arms companies will be involved in the collaborative project and will determine the form of industrial organisation for the joint project. Again, equity criteria will dominate, requiring that no single company acts as prime contractor. The result is an industrial organisation and management arrangement specific to the collaboration with the options ranging from some form of *ad hoc* industrial partnership or consortium to a new project-specific international company. Examples included the joint venture to develop and manufacture the Anglo-French Jaguar (SEPECAT for the airframe comprising Breguet and BAC) with the engine for Jaguar supplied by a joint venture of Rolls-Royce and Turbomeca; and the formation of the four-nation Eurofighter company responsible for the management of the Eurofighter programme. The efficiency of the industrial management arrangements also depend on the voting rules for decision-making with the options ranging from unanimity rules to majority voting.

A further source of collaboration inefficiencies results from the arrangements for procurement management (the demand side). The partner governments have to determine how to organise the management, monitoring and policing of the collaborative procurement. The inevitable result is the formation of international committees responsible for the procurement with their associated decision-making rules (unanimity versus majority voting). An elaborate international committee will add to transaction costs and to delays, especially where the collaboration involves new partner nations (the costs of conducting international business with strangers). Public choice analysis with its various interest groups of governments, armed forces, bureaucracies and producers appears to be a more acceptable model for explaining collaboration.

Inefficiencies also arise with similar national projects. Here, the counterfactual creates methodological problems. What is the standard of comparison between national and collaborative projects: what would have happened in the absence of collaboration? There are at least two possibilities. First, a similar or identical national project is assumed. However, often it is assumed that the similar national project is a 'perfect' programme which encounters no cost overruns, no delays and no performance shortfalls. Such 'perfect' national programmes do not exist and all high technology arms projects encounter cost, schedule and performance problems. In some cases, national projects are based on work sharing where some work is allocated to high unemployment areas. National procurement agencies are also far from perfect, subject to delays and changes in procurement policy.

Nor will a nation involved in a collaborative project develop a similar national programme which can be used as a comparator. However, comparisons can be made between similar national projects developed in *other* nations. For example, comparisons can be made between a collaborative project and similar US projects. Examples include comparisons between the collaborative Typhoon aircraft and similar US combat aircraft (e.g. F-15; F-16; F-18; F-22; F-35). Or, comparisons can be made between a collaborative project and similar European national projects: for example, between Typhoon and the national Gripen and Rafale aircraft.

Various performance indicators are needed for any comparisons. Possible examples include total development costs and unit production costs, development time scales and exports as an indicator of international competitiveness. Most performance indicators have their limitations. Data might not be available in the public domain, especially cost data. Development time scales seem an attractive indicator but there are problems of definition. For example, the starting point of a project might vary according to definitions; the date of first flight might reflect aircraft at differing stages of development (e.g. without avionics); and entry into service might also reflect aircraft which might not be combat ready. Even exports have their limitations: their prices might reflect subsidies and financial assistance to the buying nation and might include varying amounts and types of offsets.

Some of the complexities of assessing collaborative arms projects are shown in Table 5.5. Collaborative arms projects differ and include a range of aircraft, helicopter and missile types, different partner nations, different industrial arrangements and different procurement management systems. European defence collaboration for missiles is organised around a single European company namely, MBDA. For completeness, Table 5.5 presents two European national comparators, namely, the Swedish Gripen and French Rafale combat aircraft. Both these combat aircraft demonstrate that Europe has the technical and industrial capability to undertake the national development and production of a modern technically advanced aircraft and to demonstrate their international competitiveness through export orders. These facts confirm that France and Sweden were willing to

Table 5.5 Examples of major aerospace collaborative programmes

Project	*Date of service entry*	*Partner nations*	*Industrial organisation*	*Final assembly*	*Total output*	*Exports*
Typhoon	2003	Germany; Italy; Spain; UK	Eurofighter (airframe); Eurojet (engine)	Germany; Italy; Spain; UK	623	151
A400M	2013	Belgium; France; Germany; Lux; Spain; Turkey; UK	Airbus Military (airframe); Europrop (engine); OCCAR (procurement)	France; Germany; Spain; UK	174	4
Tiger	2005	France; Germany	Airbus Helicopters	France; Germany	286	46
NH90	2007	France; Germany; Italy; Netherlands	NH Industries; NAHEMA (procurement)	France; Germany; Italy; Netherlands	543	227
MBDA	2001	France; Germany; Italy; UK	MBDA—multi-national missile company	France; Germany; Italy; UK	NA	NA
Gripen	1997	Sweden	Saab	Sweden	427	153
Rafale	2001	France	Dassault	France	493	198
Tempest	2035 (estimated)	UK; Italy; Sweden; MBDA	BAE; Rolls-Royce; Leonardo; MBDA; Sweden	To be announced		
Future Combat Air System (FCAS)	2040 (estimated)	France; Germany; Spain	Dassault; Airbus; Indra Sistemas; Safran; MTU; Thales; MBDA	To be announced		

Notes: (i) Typhoon is a combat aircraft; A400M is an airlifter; Tiger is an attack helicopter and the NH90 is a multi-purpose helicopter. Gripen and Rafale are national combat aircraft shown as comparators; (ii) output and exports are volume figures (units), including orders and estimated output. Numbers for Gripen include E/F types; also 26 Gripen were leased from Sweden to Czech Republic and Hungary and were not included in the export figures; (iii) NAHEMA is NATO Helicopter Management Agency for procurement of NH90 helicopter; (iv) MBDA date is for formation of the European company. NA is not available: output data not available for different types of missiles; (v) Tempest and FCAS are both planned collaborative future European fighter aircraft. At the time of writing, no more details were available pay the price of independence. In fact, by 2020, the collaborative Typhoon had achieved a larger total output than each of Gripen and Rafale but its export numbers were lower than Rafale. Interestingly, if the nations involved in Gripen, Rafale and Typhoon had combined their orders and acquired one type, there would have been one development bill and a production run of over 1500 units of one type (compared with a maximum production run of over 600 units for the Typhoon). Duplicate development projects also are likely in the future. European nations are currently developing duplicate future combat aircraft (FCAS and Tempest). Critics of collaboration favour the US model based on the F-35 programme: they suggest a single prime contractor with a few partners, say, two partners (BAE Systems and Northrop Grumman on the F-35) so reducing the transaction costs of collaboration.

The Transaction Costs of Collaboration

The various sources of inefficiency outlined above can be presented in terms of the additional transaction costs of collaboration. Transaction costs reflect the costs of 'doing business with strangers' in the form of different partners and different industrial organisations. Transaction costs are the costs of creating, running and monitoring the multi-national organisation. Complex contracts are inevitable in such international organisations: they are incomplete contracts which allow agents opportunities for pursuing their self-interest. Each partner nation will seek business for its national champions, including favourable work shares especially of high technology work. Bargaining will lead to games of bluff, chicken and brinksmanship with nations threatening to withdraw from the programme. Collaboration has further attractions to the participants, namely, the benefits of international travel to attend meetings of procurement staffs and industrialists. Such behaviour is predicted by public choice analysis.

What is the possible magnitude of collaboration inefficiencies? Two guidelines are available. First, the *square root rule* for development costs suggests that compared with a national project, the development costs on a collaborative project can be estimated by applying the square root of the number of partner nations. On this basis, the development costs of a collaboration comprising four equal partner nations might be twice the costs for a national project. These total development costs are shared between the partner nations so that the costs per nation will be lower than for a national project, but the cost savings are lower than predicted by the ideal or perfect collaboration scenario. Second, a similar guideline applies to development time-scales. This suggests that compared with a similar national project, delays on collaborative projects can be estimated by applying the *cube root* of the number of partner nations in the collaboration. For example, an eight nation collaboration might take twice as long as a national project (Hartley and Braddon 2014).

These guidelines are difficult to operationalise. An alternative approach to assessing collaborative projects focuses on their cost overruns, delays and performance shortfalls. Table 5.6 presents some UK examples based on comparisons between collaborative projects and national ventures. This is a limited sample of projects but it shows some national projects with higher cost increases compared with collaborative projects and similar delays, although the collaborative A400M airlifter was subject to substantial delays.

The collaborative A400M airlifter is an interesting example involving a seven nation collaboration making it one of the largest international ventures based on the number of partner nations. It was developed by a division of Airbus (Airbus Military; now known as Airbus Defence and Space) with procurement managed by OCCAR. Originally, it was expected that Airbus with its international reputation as a world leader in large civil jet airliners would have been able to develop the A400M successfully. In fact, the A400M encountered major schedule, cost and technical problems. Its

Table 5.6 Costs and performance for UK Projects, 2015

Project	*Original estimated costs (£mn)*	*Latest cost figures (£mn)*	*Cost increase (%)*	*Delays (mths)*
A400M	2238	2710	+21	+79
Typhoon	15,173	17,341	+14	+54
Astute submarines 1–3	2233	3536	+58	+58
Aircraft Carriers	3541	6212	+75	+31
Total UK Projects (n = 17)	60,281	65,833	+9	+29

Source: HCP 488 (2015)

Notes: (i) A400M and Typhoon are European collaborative aircraft. Astute is a nuclear-powered submarine and the Aircraft Carriers are for two ships; (ii) total UK Projects is based on 17 UK major defence equipment projects for 2015. Latest costs are at 2015; (iii) data based on National Audit Office Major Projects Report. After 2015, NAO changed to reporting on MoD 10 year Equipment Plans, no longer publishing Major Projects Reports first flight was originally planned for 2008 but took place in December 2009. Service delivery was planned for 2009 but was delayed until August 2013. Costs have risen. There was a government bail-out of Euros 3.5 billion for the project in 2010 and Airbus confirmed a Euros 2.2 billion charge on the A400M for 2016 (estimated at Euros 6 billion in *total* charges for Airbus). Technical and operational problems have also arisen. Technical problems affected the engine and its propeller gearboxes as well as fuselage cracks. Operational problems arose over in-flight refuelling for helicopters. Cost increases led to reductions in planned orders from 25 to 22 for the UK, from 60 to 53 for Germany whilst South Africa cancelled its export order. Critics suggested that Airbus under-estimated the engine problems, especially for an inexperienced engine consortium. Overall, the A400M has been regarded as an unsatisfactory programme with an unsatisfactory contract and by no means an example of a successful collaboration (Hartley and Belin 2020).

Conclusion

Efforts to create a Single European Market are constrained by the existence of independent nation states. Here, the US model is informative with its Single Market for defence equipment and a single US Army, Navy, Air Force and Marine Corps. The European equivalent requires a federal state with a single European Army, Navy and Air Force, able to reduce duplication in development and large enough to achieve economies of scale and learning in defence markets.

The challenge of improving efficiency in NATO defence markets is firmly located in the European Union. The USA does not have the problems of fragmentation, duplication and small scale which typify European defence markets leading to NATO being an inefficient defence market. NATO inefficiency forms one of its major future challenges. Whilst the focus is on Europe, it does not follow that the US defence market comprising its armed forces and defence industries is a model of efficiency.

In an era when defence equipment is costly and where costs continue to rise, military alliances offer prospects for economising on defence budgets. As a military alliance, NATO can improve the efficiency of its armed forces and defence industries. Economic theory suggests two principles for a more efficient organisation of its armed forces and defence industries. First, the principle of specialisation by comparative advantage offering gains from competitive international trade. Second, gains from volume production in defence industries reflecting economies of scale and learning. After 70 years, NATO remains an inefficient organisation for providing armed forces and supplying defence equipment. But inefficiency is only one of the future challenges for NATO.

References

Augustine, N. (1987). *Augustine's Laws*. London: Penguin.

EC. (2016, November). EC Communication from the Commission to the European Parliament, the European Council, the European Council of the European Economic and Social Committee and the Committee of the Regions: *The European Defence Action Plan*, European Commission, Brussels.

EC. (2009, July). *Defence Procurement Directive 2009/81/EC*. Brussels: European Commission.

EDA. (2007, May). *EDA Note for the Steering Board No 2007/08, European Defence Technological and Industrial Base Strategy*. Brussels: EDA.

EDA. (2016, June). *National Defence Data 2013–2014 of the 27 EDA Member States*. Brussels: European Defence Agency.

Hartley, K. (2020). Rising Costs: Augustine Revisited. *Defence and Peace Economics, 31*(4), 434–442.

Hartley, K., & Belin, J. (Eds.). (2020). *The Economics of the Global Defence Industry*. London: Routledge.

Hartley, K., & Braddon, D. (2014). Collaborative Projects and the Number of Partner Nations. *Defence and Peace Economics, 25*(6), 535–548.

HCP 488. (2015, October). *Major Projects Report 2015 and the Equipment Plan 2015 to 2025*. London: TSO.

Kirkpatrick, D. L. (1995). The Rising Unit Costs of Defence—The Reasons and the Results. *Defence and Peace Economics, 6*(4), 263–288.

Pugh, P. G. (2007). *Source Book of Defence Equipment Costs*. London: Dandy Books.

SIPRI. (2020). *Arms Production Database*. Stockholm: Stockholm International Peace Research Institute.

CHAPTER 6

Future Challenges

Abstract The survival of NATO depends on its ability to respond to future challenges from new threats. NATO's distinctive attributes are an established alliance, an experienced command structure and capable military forces. Alternatives to NATO are assessed. Proposals for improving efficiency and enlargement are reviewed. Future battlefields and the future of the defence firm are explored.

Keywords Economic and military benefits • Defence economics • Enlargement • Standardisation

Introduction: Where Next?

NATO faces major future challenges which will determine its survival. The future is uncertain and no one can predict it accurately: today's winners might well be tomorrow's losers. Even if NATO survives, for how long and in what form? Will there be further enlargements (with whom?); what are the future benefits of NATO and what will be the future threats? These issues are addressed in this chapter. It shows how economic analysis can be used to provide insights into the future of NATO and the alternatives.

K. Hartley, *NATO at 70*,
https://doi.org/10.1007/978-3-030-54395-2_6

New Threats

The future survival of NATO will partly depend on its ability to adapt and respond to new threats. China is an obvious and emerging superpower rival for the USA. At the end of World War II, the USA was the planet's dominant nation; later it was victor of the Cold War. By 2020, the US global primacy appeared to be ending with China emerging as a superpower rival reflected in its economic growth, the size of its GDP, foreign investment and military spending some of which is on high technology defence equipment (e.g. aircraft carriers; combat aircraft; space satellites). At the same time, there is a view that no US major politician dares to tell their own people that their global supremacy is coming to an end (Mahbubani 2020). The US position on its future world power role will determine the future of NATO.

There will be other threats to NATO. These include the revival of Russia as a world power and its rivalry with both China and the USA. Other states will emerge as world powers over the next 70 years: these are not yet known but will eventually emerge. Further new threats will come from new technology and the nations which develop this technology. Again, this new technology and its origin nations have yet to emerge; but NATO has to be capable of responding and adapting to such threats from new and unknown technology. Much depends on defence and civil R&D spending in the USA and other NATO nations. Here, civil R&D spending might provide access to new technologies which might become future military threats to NATO.

Pandemics are a major threat: they have the ability to radically affect the performance of economies. The Coronavirus pandemic of 2020 resulted in the 'lockdown' of national economies with major implications for international travel, tourism, hospitality and health industries. Economies required massive increases in public spending to avoid recessions and to provide funds for the unemployed. In the long-term, such increased government pandemic public spending might mean reductions in other government spending including cuts in defence spending.

Climate change is another new threat. It might, for example, lead to resource shortages which become a cause of conflict (e.g. droughts and access to water resources). Other new threats include cyber warfare and the space domain. Space is a completely new domain for the development of weapons. The use of space for satellites and surveillance means that it cannot be ignored by Armed Forces. The destruction of a nation's satellites gives an attacker a military advantage: it destroys an enemy's communications and surveillance capability. Overall, there is no shortage of threats both known and unknown which can be used to justify the retention of NATO. But more is required to justify its continued existence. Is the current form of NATO adequate or are there better alternatives where better embraces lower cost and/or more effective solutions? To survive, NATO has to demonstrate that as a collective military alliance it is the least-cost solution to providing protection and that it is a lower-cost solution than other national defence policies.

New Roles

New threats might lead NATO to new roles and there is no shortage of possibilities for new missions. NATO has some distinctive attributes. It is an established international military alliance with an experienced command structure and trained and capable armed forces. These are valuable assets with a range of alternative uses. Examples include expanded roles in crisis management, humanitarian and disaster relief. Other opportunities include international peace-keeping and enforcing. Recreating these NATO assets and attributes would take time and be costly. But time and costs are not necessarily reasons for retaining NATO: national solutions might be more cost-effective. The case for NATO is based on the benefits of international collective action convincingly outweighing its costs.

NATO Military and Economic Benefits

NATO continues to offer military and economic benefits. It remains a military alliance providing collective security through its Article 5 military multiplier in the form of an attack on one member being regarded as an attack on all members. Economics enters the equation since the NATO alliance provides defence to its members at a lower cost than the alternative of national independence. On this basis, NATO is a 'win-win' for all members.

For the Europeans, consider the alternatives to NATO. First, Europe could develop an independent strategic nuclear deterrent under its own control and rely upon it to deter other nations from attacking Europe. Second, each Member State could rely on its conventional forces to provide adequate national defence. The absence of a military alliance would mean no national contribution to collective defence and the end of burden-sharing debates.

Nations would have to assess the costs and risks of non-NATO. Consider the option of a European strategic nuclear deterrent. This will be costly but could be based on the French (and UK) nuclear deterrent. It is likely to be a small nuclear force based in Europe and close geographically to Russia so that protecting these forces from a Russian surprise attack will be extremely costly and difficult militarily. Europe's vulnerability to a Russian nuclear attack might also be greater since the probability that the US strategic nuclear force will respond will be lower once the USA has withdrawn from any Article 5 commitments. Effectively, Europe would be trading a small increase in its nuclear threat to Russia for a massive decrease in the threat to Russia from the US nuclear deterrent. If Europe is unwilling to rely on an independent nuclear deterrent, it might prefer conventional forces but still rely on US nuclear forces to deter war (assuming a US willingness to provide its nuclear deterrent). Without a military alliance, this is a risky option but attractively cheap.

In assessing a non-NATO option, European nations will evaluate the costs and benefits of alternative defence policies. These range over strategic nuclear capabilities to various types of conventional military capabilities. Here, the options include 'strong' conventional forces (modern army, navy and air force) or role specialisation within a European defence force. Assessing the costs of these options is relatively easy; but the benefits assessment is much more problematic. Assessing the benefits of defence requires some measure of defence output. Typically, economists refer to defence output in such broad terms as peace, protection and security; but any cost-benefit analysis of defence policy options requires a money valuation to be placed on defence output. No such money valuation exists. Instead, the traditional solution was to assume that inputs equalled outputs which is not a satisfactory solution. Alternative approaches have focused on the military capabilities of various levels of defence spending. For example, a defence budget of $X billion might 'buy' the capability to deploy specific numbers of soldiers, tanks, warships and combat aircraft in some overseas region for a specified period of time. But, no money valuation is attached to such a military capability so that the costs and benefits of various defence policy options cannot be evaluated and the defence economics problem remains.

The Defence Economics Problem

A future of rising unit costs and either falling or stable defence budgets in real terms means that difficult defence choices cannot be avoided. The Augustine scenario of a single tank army, single ship navy and Battlestar Galactica for the air force might become reality for all NATO forces. Costs, economics and efficiency will become more important in the future NATO. Cost and budget pressures will lead national military forces to search for efficiency improvements. Continued membership of a military alliance appears cost-effective and there are further opportunities for efficiency improvements *within* alliances. Within an alliance, internal efficiency can be improved through standardisation and improved collaboration.

Standardisation

Weapons standardisation is attractive to a military alliance. It involves two or more members of an alliance using identical equipment. Standardisation increases the military effectiveness of the alliance armed forces. For example, the armies of two or more members of an alliance would all use the same tanks so allowing them to be re-armed with common ammunition and repaired at any military base throughout the alliance. Aircraft would take-off in one country and land at an airfield in another Member State where they could be refuelled and re-armed ready for another mission.

Economics predicts that standardisation provides industrial benefits of lower unit costs from large-scale production. Larger orders allow fixed development costs to be spread over larger outputs and greater quantities lead to lower unit production costs from economies of scale and learning (see Fig. 5.1). Whilst standardisation is attractive, it encounters barriers of nationalism as each Member State prefers independence with the ability to use its armed forces independently with the reliability of re-supply in conflict. Furthermore, diversity of weapons and non-standardisation has some military benefits since it presents different threats to rival nations in a conflict.

Weapons standardisation can be achieved in various ways. Member States could all import the same type of weapon, such as NATO Member States buying US equipment (e.g. F-16 and F-35 combat aircraft). Or, a degree of standardisation can be achieved through two or more nations agreeing to cooperative purchasing of the same equipment or through international collaboration on the supply-side.

Improving Efficiency: Alternative Models of Collaboration

There are at least three alternative models for European arms collaboration. First, the US F-35 model; second, the Airbus model and third, the economics model.

The US F-35 Lightning II programme is one model. The US government is the major buyer of this multi-role combat aircraft for the three US services. The F-35 resulted from a competition between Lockheed Martin and Boeing with Lockheed Martin winning the competition for the Joint Strike Fighter (JSF). The project is mostly funded by the US government with further contributions to its development costs from international partners. The UK is the only Level 1 partner contributing some 10% of the original planned development costs. Level 2 partners include Italy with a contribution of $1 billion and the Netherlands with a contribution of $800 million. Level 3 partners making smaller financial contributions to the project include Australia, Canada, Denmark, Norway and Turkey.

Lockheed Martin is the prime contractor with Northrop Grumman and BAE Systems (UK) as major industrial partners. Northrop Grumman has a work share of about 25% on the project, including work on the centre fuselage. BAE Systems has been awarded a 13% to 15% work share on each aircraft (comprising the rear section) with estimates suggesting support for some 25,000 UK jobs. But the project has not been problem-free. There have been cost overruns estimated at $163 billion, delays of 7 years as well as performance problems. Critics have suggested that the project is too costly to cancel!

Airbus is another alternative model for European arms collaboration. Many critics regard Airbus as a classic example of a successful European collaboration. It is a world-class firm forming a duopoly with Boeing in the world market for the supply of large civil jet airliners. Airbus is an international company with two major partner nations (France and Germany with Spain as a minor partner). In comparison, Boeing is a one nation and privately owned company which is not state-owned and is not subject to governance by two or more partner nations. Airbus has achieved US scales of output for its major jet airliners to become a world-class firm and rival to Boeing: it demonstrates that multinational collaboration can be successful.

There are, however, differences between Airbus and other European military aerospace collaborations. First, Airbus market success has been in civil aircraft markets where there are large numbers of buyers, many being privately owned profit-seeking firms. In contrast, arms collaborations involve a few procurement agencies and their national partner governments funded on cost-based contracts providing soft budget constraints. Second, Airbus specialises in civil jet aircraft which are not as technically advanced as military combat aircraft. Third, Airbus is a European company with a permanent existence compared with the typical *ad hoc* project-specific consortium for European arms collaboration. The result is an established European company which acts as a single prime contractor representing companies in three nations. Finally, Airbus has a small number of partner nations which might demonstrate the success of collaborations based on small numbers of partners. But the Airbus model is not all success. The performance of its Defence Division on the A400M airlifter has been far from successful (Hartley and Braddon 2014).

Economics offers guidelines for an alternative model of efficient arms collaboration. Economic theory predicts that efficient solutions require profit-seeking private firms operating in competitive markets, where efficiency results from competition in product markets and the 'policing' and monitoring role of capital markets (i.e. threats of takeovers and bankruptcy). This suggests some radical changes to existing arrangements for European arms collaboration. Competition is required to select a single prime contractor which should be a private firm subject to hard budget constraints (i.e. a fixed price contract). The prime contractor would be responsible for selecting its major suppliers with work allocated on competitive criteria rather than *juste retour*. Partner nations would buy shares in the project similar to the US F-35 project but there would be a lead nation (c.f. USA for F-35). The economic principles for efficient arms collaboration are clear but politics will intervene. Nations will not agree to a single lead nation and a single prime contractor for a project: all partner nations will demand a major role in project management and the involvement of their national champion firms.

Future European Defence Industrial Policy

European defence industrial policy has two components, namely, the creation of a Single Market for defence equipment and the formation of a European Defence Technology and Industrial Base (EDTIB). Immediately, there are potential conflicts between these aims. A genuinely competitive Single Market will conflict with the aim of creating an EDTIB. Competition will allocate scarce resources between different regions and nations within the Single Market but this might mean some regions losing defence technology and production capabilities and such losses might be regarded as politically and socially undesirable. Nor is the concept of an EDTIB problem-free. Its key components and capabilities have to be identified and agreed between partner nations. For example, decisions are needed about the location of the major design, development and production facilities for air, land and sea systems (which nations?) with the locations likely to be determined by governments. Funding has to be arranged and agreed between Member States which will raise new burden-sharing debates. Also, financial support has to be provided during troughs in development and production work for defence plants. Solutions to troughs in defence work include the development of cheap prototypes and technology demonstrators, limited production orders and the mothballing of plants. Inevitably, the Single Market and EDTIB will be dominated by the desire of governments, bureaucracies and producer groups for '*managed competition*' (managed by vested interest groups) which public choice analysis predicts will depart from economic efficiency principles.

Despite political constraints, continued pressures on defence budgets mean that economic efficiency principles cannot be ignored. There are considerable opportunities for improving the efficiency of NATO and European arms collaboration and their Armed Forces. The efficiency of arms collaboration can be improved by applying the lessons from Airbus and the US F-35 programme. Also, collaboration might be extended beyond acquisition to include all aspects of a project's life-cycle. Examples include extending collaboration to include training, repair and maintenance as well as mid-life updates. Collaboration might also be extended to include nations from outside Europe (e.g. Australia; Brazil; Canada; Japan; South Africa; South Korea).

Opportunities exist for improving the efficiency of NATO and EU Armed Forces. Examples include extending military outsourcing and avoiding wasteful duplication in acquiring, owning and sharing costly military assets (e.g. anti-ballistic missile defence; duplication of nuclear forces; duplication of aircraft carriers; air tankers; specialist surveillance aircraft). More radical changes arise from applying the economic principles of substitution and specialisation by comparative advantage. Substitution possibilities include reserve forces replacing regular forces; civilians replacing military personnel; drones replacing manned combat aircraft; and nuclear forces replacing conventional forces. Applied to the EU's Armed Forces, the economic principle of specialisation by comparative advantage would mean Member States providing those Armed Forces where they have a comparative advantage. Germany might specialise in armoured forces; France and the UK might provide aircraft carriers and nuclear forces; and the Netherlands might provide escort vessels for the aircraft carriers. Trust is a major constraint on achieving such specialisation: in a conflict, will allies providing the specialist military capability turn-up? Trust is also a problem when sharing costly military assets. Sharing appears attractive but it ignores some fundamental problems. Who will 'own' the asset and have the 'right' to use it in a conflict; and how will the costs of ownership be shared between the 'owners' (a burden-sharing issue)? Next, there are future challenges for NATO in enlargement through possible new members.

NATO Enlargement: New Members and the Limits to Membership?

For analysis of NATO expansion, the alliance can be regarded as a club where Member States join so long as membership is expected to be worthwhile. Benefits and costs are viewed from the perspective of existing members and from the perspective of the new member. For existing members, benefits might take the form of the new entrant providing additional military forces supplying a range of defence outputs (joint products) and contributing to joint costs. New members also involve costs in the form of additional risks of conflict and increased transaction costs associated with more Member States. Decision-making rules might have to be changed with choices between unanimity and majority voting rules. Whilst recognition of benefits and costs is a useful guide to expansion, it provides no indication of whether there is a limit to the size of NATO and what that limit might be.

New members involve additional costs and benefits which also extend to *existing* members. If all existing members and the new entrant view an enlargement as providing net benefits, then the admission of the new ally should proceed. Net benefits require an assessment of both additional costs and additional benefits for two groups, namely, existing members and the new entrant. NATO provision for enlargement involves Article 10 of the Treaty which allows entry to any European state which furthers the principles of the Treaty and contributes to the security of the Atlantic area. Potential new members might include Bosnia and Herzegovina, Georgia, Ukraine, Serbia, Finland and Sweden. Some of these potential applicants are also members of NATO's Partnership for Peace programme.

Economic theory offers guidelines on enlargement, carefully distinguishing between new and existing members. The benefits for a *new* member might include increased peace and stability, democratic reforms and improved relations between neighbouring states. Further benefits for the new member might include greater protection provided by an international military alliance. A new member also brings benefits to existing members through, for example, increased arms sales by NATO arms producers, especially the USA. Increased arms sales lead to economies of scale and learning resulting in lower unit costs and lower unit prices. A new member might also contribute additional protection for existing members. Established members will also receive a monetary gain from the greater sharing of NATO common infrastructure costs associated with the new member.

Membership of NATO involves an entry path starting with a Membership Action Plan (MAP) where a country has to declare an interest in joining the alliance. A prior entry point is the Partnership for Peace programme (PfP), created in 1994 involving partnerships between NATO and countries from the Euro-Atlantic area, the Mediterranean and Gulf region. There are also individual dialogue-cooperation relationships with countries such as Australia, Japan, South Korea and New Zealand (Partners across the globe). Countries wishing to join NATO are required to participate in the PfP as a prerequisite to joining the Membership Action Plan.

New entry and expansion involves costs. For new members, there are increased costs where NATO membership requires force modernisation, additional training, standardisation expenses and the costs of modernising military bases. Direct enlargement costs include upgrading command, control, communications and intelligence facilities and extending NATO infrastructure (e.g. pipelines; airfields; ports). New members will also be required to contribute towards NATO's common infrastructure costs and to provide military bases for use by NATO forces. Only those costs which arise from NATO expansion should be included: costs which would be incurred without NATO entry should not be included as an expansion cost (Belkin 2019).

There are three further costs which are difficult to measure but might be the most important. First, a new ally might increase the risks of conflict for the whole alliance. For example, a new member might provoke Russia. Second, expansion might lead to greater *force thinning* as a given size of conventional forces is allocated to defend longer borders. Third, expansion means that decision-making may be slower and more difficult to reach a conclusion. For example, a larger alliance makes it more difficult to reach speedy and agreed conclusions on crisis management where military action requires a rapid response. This raises the more general question of the ideal size and composition of NATO. Economists suggest that the ideal economic size of NATO occurs where the additional costs of enlargement equal the additional benefits for existing members and the new entrant (Sandler and Hartley 1999).

There are no published studies of the costs and benefits of NATO expansion. In view of the expansions which have occurred, this is surprising and a major flaw and deficiency in any economic assessment of NATO. Benefits are difficult to measure in money terms: how do you value peace and security? However, one economic benefit has been identified. It has been estimated that NATO membership and partnerships have had a positive impact on a country's economic growth (Gonzalez et al. 2019).

Costs of NATO expansion are relatively easier to identify, measure and value. For example, studies have estimated the costs of US troops in Europe. A 2018 study estimated the costs of the US military presence in Europe at between $24 billion and £35.8 billion per year (IISS 2019); and a 2019 US study estimated the costs of US military forces in Europe at $10.4 billion per annum (Belkin 2019). The cost estimates vary widely depending on the definitions of costs. Moreover, these are estimates of the costs of US military forces in Europe only which do not indicate the full extent of costs borne by all NATO allies.

In terms of defence objectives, some of the NATO enlargements are difficult to justify. They appear to reflect an objective of maximising the number of members rather than increasing net protection. For new entrants, the question needs to be asked: what does the new member add to NATO collective defence and at what cost? Decision-making rules also need to be reviewed. Not all members are equal and a rule of one member one vote and majority voting means that the dominant member militarily can be easily out-voted by a number of smaller states with small military forces. Similarly, choices are needed between majority voting and a unanimity rule. Unanimity means that all members have to agree on a choice but the costs and time needed to reach a unanimous decision for 30 members might be substantial with an inconclusive outcome seriously weakening the effectiveness of a military alliance needing to respond rapidly to a crisis situation.

NATO expansion is one dimension of size, but the possibility arises of exit from NATO. Withdrawal from NATO involves Article 13 of the Treaty. The procedure for exit requires that the departing country informs the USA which then informs other members. After a one year wait, the departing country formally leaves and ceases to be a member. Exit from NATO or any military alliance will depend on the costs and benefits of exit versus remaining a member. One determinant of exit or remaining might be the likely form of the future battlefield.

Future Battlefields

NATO faces massive uncertainties about the future battlefield over the next 50 to 70 years. Will future conflicts be similar to recent battles or will they be radically different? History suggests the possibility of massive changes. The Second World War was drastically different from the First World War (e.g. the Second had a major role for aircraft, tanks and submarines compared with WWI). Massive change will need corresponding changes in Armed Forces and the end of some traditional military roles: for instance, manned tanks might be replaced by remotely controlled armoured vehicles.

Technical change has typified warfare. Bows and arrows were replaced by rifles; cannons replaced castles; sail-powered galleons were replaced by battleships and aircraft carriers; nuclear weapons replaced large concentrations of troops; and inter-continental ballistic rockets and cruise missiles replaced large conventional bomber forces (c.f. RAF Bomber Command in WWII). Nations which fail to introduce new military technologies might be defeated in conflict. Even non-state actors such as terrorist groups, are changing and adjusting to new technology. Following the wars in the Persian Gulf, Afghanistan and Iraq, terrorist groups concluded that it was not sensible to confront the USA and its Western allies on their own terms. Instead, the West's enemies have responded to its military superiority in air warfare by learning new lessons, such as how to communicate effectively with their friends without alerting western intelligence agencies (Kilcullen 2020).

To illustrate future battlefield prospects, consider two scenarios, namely, the Augustine weapons scenario and the cheap drones scenario. The Augustine scenario continues the historical trend of ever more technically complex and costlier weapons with rising real unit costs. These weapons are so expensive that there are forecasts of single ship navies, single tank armies and Battlestar Galactica for the air force (Augustine 1987). Battlefields will be automated with robot soldiers and remotely controlled air, land, sea and space weapons. Augustine weapons will be so costly that future wars will be short duration, high intensity conflicts. Armed Forces will have to fight with their existing stocks of weapons since replacing stocks via new production will take considerable time. For defence industries, there will be fewer new development projects and shorter production runs reflecting smaller quantities for the Armed Forces.

The alternative scenario is one of swarms of cheap drones. These can be bought off-the-shelf (e.g. in toy shops) by terrorists and other violent extremist groups (Lyle 2019). They enable terrorists and non-state groups to acquire air power cheaply without the need for all the supporting inputs required for a modern air force. Drones are cheap, priced at $200–500, with relatively large numbers of suppliers. Drones are easier to operate, easy to modify and cheaper to buy which makes them the opposite of the costly and rising unit cost of the Augustine weapons. The drones scenario is especially worrying with anti-drone technology being so costly: interceptor missiles in Israel's Iron Dome cost US $100,000 and are a costly solution to threats from US $200 drones (Lyle 2019). Of course, the future battlefield might combine both scenarios with costly Augustine weapons managing and controlling fleets of cheap drones. Next, questions arise about the future of the defence firm in NATO.

The Future NATO Defence Firm

At the outset, questions arise about whether the NATO defence firm has a future: will it exist in 50–70 years time in, say, 2070–2090? Long-term forecasts are most likely to be wrong but some broad generalisations are possible. There will continue to be a need for defence firms so long as military threats remain. Barring an unprecedented outbreak of world peace, defence firms will be needed to respond to threats to national peace and security. Even with world peace, there will remain a limited demand for weapons from international peace-keepers.

The future defence firm will be different. It will be as different as today's defence firms are as different from those of 1945 and 1914. For example, in 1914, the aircraft industry was a new entrant industry which was just emerging; by 1945, it was building rockets and early versions of cruise missiles (V-1 and V-2 rockets); and by 1969 it had become an aerospace industry building rockets for lunar travel.

For the future, there will be a smaller number of larger defence firms. These are likely to be international firms with sales of a range of air, land, sea and space systems involving mergers between US and European defence firms. The future NATO defence firm will probably be 'too big to fail.' Giant firms will also create regulatory challenges for national governments as they have to determine the prices and profitability of major defence contracts. Nor can national governments ignore the future challenge and costs of retaining a national defence industrial base. National defence industries will face troughs in development and production work and the costs of retaining defence industrial capacity during such troughs. Policy options include funding technology demonstrators, awarding limited production contracts to retain capacity or 'mothballing' industrial facilities. None of these options are costless.

The future NATO defence firm will diversify by acquiring a large civil business. The aim will be to reduce a defence firm's dependence on military business and its dependence on national government as a single or major buyer. But, even more challenges arise since governments will have to decide whether they prefer competition to monopoly in national defence markets. Competition requires alternative suppliers which means either supporting a number of rival firms in national defence markets or allowing foreign firms to bid for national defence contracts.

Conclusion

The future of NATO requires three questions to be addressed. First, what is known about NATO; second, what is not known; and third, what needs to be known for making sensible public choices on the future of NATO? The answer to all three questions is that much is known, a lot is unknown and more needs to be known.

Starting with the knowns, there are considerable data on the facts about NATO. There are time-series and cross-section data by country on military expenditure, numbers of military personnel and the allocation of defence budgets between equipment, personnel and other inputs. There are also data on NATO's defence industries and its major arms firms.

There is much which remains unknown. More data are needed on the size of NATO defence industries measured by both sales and employment and on defence industry supply chains. Defence R&D data by NATO members is lacking as well data on industry and firm performance measured by labour and value-added productivity, profitability and exports. Insights into the gains from improved efficiency in NATO require data on unit cost curves for different types of weapons (e.g. combat aircraft; tanks; warships) and the impact on unit costs of larger scale production.

There is much which needs to be known. National defence markets and their procurement, competition and contracting policies need to be identified and evaluated. NATO decision-making has to be assessed for its efficiency and cost-benefit studies are needed of enlargement. An evaluation framework needs to be established and then used to evaluate applications for new entry. Comparisons of procurement policies in NATO enable the identification of those which are successful and those which are failures where the successes provide policy guidelines for further improvements in NATO efficiency.

For the future, there are a range of policy options for achieving lower costs and improving the defence effectiveness of NATO. First, a more effective military alliance would be achieved with the addition of Sweden as a new member. Other candidates as new members include Australia, Japan and South Korea all of which might be suited to respond to the emerging threat from China. Second, various options exist for improving the efficiency of NATO. These include the creation of a NATO Single Market or a Free Trade Area in defence equipment; or the creation of more efficient collaborative programmes; or strengthening the Single European Defence Equipment Market; or improving NATO's decision-making apparatus.

Economics provides an analytical framework for thinking about the future of NATO. It is valuable in raising the resource question of what are the costs of NATO and what are its benefits? It directs analysts to seek answers to questions but it does not provide answers: these are matters of judgement by analysts. Typically, economics is not the only method of analysing the future of NATO. Other disciplines are relevant including politics, strategic studies, international relations, sociology, military analysis and theology. Some of the issues for the future of NATO involve morality. For example, the morality of using nuclear weapons which can affect the future of civilisation and is as equally important as the debates about climate change.

References

Augustine, N. (1987). *Augustine's Laws*. London: Penguin Books.

Belkin, P. (2019). *Assessing NATO's Value. Congressional Research Service*. Washington, DC: US Government Printing Office.

Gonzalez, N. U., Hromcova, J., & Callado-Munoz, F. J. (2019). Defence Spending, Institutional Environment and Economic Growth: The Case of NATO. *Defence and Peace Economics, 30*(5), 525–548.

Hartley, K., & Braddon, D. (2014). Collaborative Projects and the Number of Partner Nations. *Defence and Peace Economics, 25*(6), 535–548.

IISS, (2019). *Defending Europe: Scenario Based Capability Requirements for NATO's European Members*. London: International Institute for Strategic Studies.

Kilcullen, D. (2020). *Dragons and the Snakes: How the Rest Learned to Fight the West*. London: Hurst.

Lyle, P. (2019). Air Power Proliferation: How Commercial Off-the-shelf Drones are Being Used by Violent Extrmist Organisations to Influence the Future of Warfare in the Air. *Air and Space Power Review, 22*(3), 100–121.

Mahbubani, K. (2020). *Has China Won? The Chinese Challenge to American Supremacy*. New York City: Public Affairs Books.

Sandler, T., & Hartley, K. (1999). *The Political Economy of NATO*. Cambridge: Cambridge University Press.

References

Amara, J. (2007). Evaluating NATO Long Run Defense Burdens Using Unit Root Tests. *Defence and Peace Economics, 18*(2), 157–181.

Amara, J. (2008). NATO Defense Expenditures: Common Goals or Diverging Interests? A Structural Analysis. *Defence and Peace Economics, 19*(6), 449–469.

Augustine, N. (1987). *Augustine's Laws*. London: Penguin.

Beeres, R., & Bogers, M. (2012). Ranking the Performance of European Armed Forces. *Defence and Peace Economics, 23*(1), 1–16.

Belkin, P. (2019). *Assessing NATO's Value. Congressional Research Service*. Washington, DC: US Government Printing Office.

Bitzinger, R. (1989, May). *Assessing the Conventional Balance in Europe, 1945–1975*. Santa Monica: Rand.

Buchanan, J. (1986). *Liberty, Market and the State*. London: Harvester.

Chilcott, S. J. (2016). *The Report of the Iraq Inquiry*. London: TSO.

Dannatt, R. (2016). *Boots on the Ground: Britain and Her Army since 1945*. London: Profile Books.

Dowdy, J. (2017, November). *More Tooth, Less Tail: Getting Beyond NATO's 2 Percent Rule*. London: McKinsey and Company.

Downs, A. (1957). *An Economic Theory of Democracy*. New York: Harper and Row.

EC. (2016, November). EC Communication from the Commission to the European Parliament, the European Council, the European Council of the European Economic and Social Committee and the Committee of the Regions: *The European Defence Action Plan*, European Commission, Brussels.

EC. (2009, July). *Defence Procurement Directive 2009/81/EC*. Brussels: European Commission.

K. Hartley, *NATO at 70*,
https://doi.org/10.1007/978-3-030-54395-2

EDA. (2007, May). *EDA Note for the Steering Board No 2007/08, European Defence Technological and Industrial Base Strategy*. Brussels: EDA.

EDA. (2016, June). *National Defence Data 2013–2014 of the 27 EDA Member States*. Brussels: European Defence Agency.

Ellehuus, R. (2019). *NATO at 70—Shaping the Future for the Next 70 Years*. Washington, DC: Commentary by Center for Strategic and International Studies.

Gates, W. R., & Terasawa, K. L. (2003). Reconsidering Publicness in Alliance Defence Expenditures: NATO Expansion and Burden Sharing. *Defence and Peace Economics, 14*(5), 369–383.

Gonzalez, N. U., Hromcova, J., & Callado-Munoz, F. J. (2019). Defence Spending, Institutional Environment and Economic Growth: The Case of NATO. *Defence and Peace Economics, 30*(5), 525–548.

Hartley, K. (2011). *The Economics of Defence Policy*. London: Routledge.

Hartley, K. (2018). The Profitability of Non-Competitive Defence Contracts: The UK Experience. *Defence and Peace Economics, 29*(6), 577–594.

Hartley, K. (2020). Rising Costs: Augustine Revisited. *Defence and Peace Economics, 31*(4), 434–442.

Hartley, K., & Belin, J. (Eds.). (2020). *The Economics of the Global Defence Industry*. London: Routledge.

Hartley, K., & Braddon, D. (2014). Collaborative Projects and the Number of Partner Nations. *Defence and Peace Economics, 25*(6), 535–548.

Hartley, K., & Lynk, E. (1983, February). Labour Demand and Allocation in the UK Engineering Industry: Disaggregation, Structural Change and Defence Reviews. *Scottish Journal of Political Economy, 30*(1), 42–53.

Hartley, K., & Sandler, T. (1999). NATO Burden-Sharing: Past and Future. *Journal of Peace Research, 36*(6), 665–680.

Hastings, M. (2020, March 8). The West v the Rest, Book Review by Max Hastings. *The Times*, pp. 35.

HCP 488. (2015, October). *Major Projects Report 2015 and the Equipment Plan 2015 to 2025*. London: TSO.

IISS. (2019). *Defending Europe: Scenario Based Capability Requirements for NATO's European Members*. London: International Institute for Strategic Studies.

Kilcullen, D. (2020). *Dragons and the Snakes: How the Rest Learned to Fight the West*. London: Hurst.

Kirkpatrick, D. L. (1995). The Rising Unit Costs of Defence—The Reasons and the Results. *Defence and Peace Economics, 6*(4), 263–288.

Lindley-French, J. (2020, May 13). *Reflecting on NATO 2030*, Website.

Lyle, P. (2019). Air Power Proliferation: How Commercial Off-the-shelf Drones are Being Used by Violent Extrmist Organisations to Influence the Future of Warfare in the Air. *Air and Space Power Review, 22*(3), 100–121.

Lynk, E., & Hartley, K. (1985). Input Demands and Elasticities in UK Defence Industries. *International Journal of Industrial Organization, 3*, 71–83.

Mahbubani, K. (2020). *Has China Won? The Chinese Challenge to American Supremacy*. New York City: Public Affairs Books.

Mueller, D. C. (1989). *Public Choice II*. Cambridge: Cambridge University Press.

NATO. (2019a, December). *Funding NATO*. Brussels: North Atlantic Treaty Organization.

NATO. (2019b). *Press Release, 25th June, 2019, Defence Expenditure of NATO countries (2012–2019)*. Brussels: NATO.

Niskanen, W. (1971). *Bureaucracy and Representative Government*. Chicago: Aldine-Atherton.

Olson, M. (1965). *The Logic of Collective Action*. Cambridge, MA: Harvard University Press.

Olson, M., & Zeckhauser, R. (1966). An Economic Theory of Alliances. *Review of Economics and Statistics, 48*(3), 266–279.

Pugh, P. G. (2007). *Source Book of Defence Equipment Costs*. London: Dandy Books.

Sandler, T. (1992). *Collective Action: Theory and Applications*. Ann Arbor: University of Michigan Press.

Sandler, T. (2005). NATO Benefits, Burdens and Borders: Comment. *Defence and Peace Economics, 16*(4), 317–321.

Sandler, T., & Hartley, K. (1999). *The Political Economy of NATO*. Cambridge: Cambridge University Press.

Sandler, T., & Hartley, K. (2001). Economics of Alliances: The Lessons for Collective Action. *Journal of Economic Literature, XXXIX*(3), 869–896.

SIPRI. (2020). *Arms Production Database*. Stockholm: Stockholm International Peace Research Institute.

Siqueira, K., & Sandler, T. (2001). Models of Alliances: Internalizing Externalities and Financing. *Defence and Peace Economics, 12*(3), 249–270.

Solomon, B. (2004). NATO Burden Sharing Revisited. *Defence and Peace Economics, 15*(3), 251–258.

Spohr, K. (2019). 1989–2019: How the End of the Cold War Shaped Today's World, An Interview with Kristina Spohr. *RUSI Journal, 164*(7), 68–76.

Tisdell, C., & Hartley, K. (2008). *Microeconomic Policy*. Cheltenham: Elgar.

Index

K. Hartley, *NATO at 70*,
https://doi.org/10.1007/978-3-030-54395-2

The manufacturer's authorised representative in the EU is Springer Nature Customer Service Centre GmbH, Europaplatz 3, 69115 Heidelberg, Germany. If you have any concerns regarding our products, please contact ProductSafety@springernature.com

Printed and bound by CPI Group (UK) Ltd, Croydon, CR0 4YY

30/09/2026

02225470-0001